Teaching Reading to All Learners Including Those with Complex Needs

Learning to read and having access to a rich reading curriculum has a huge impact upon us both emotionally and academically, so how can we ensure that it is seen as an entitlement of all learners, including those defined as having profound and multiple learning difficulties (PMLD) and the most complex needs?

This accessible book provides professionals with the knowledge and confidence to develop reading for all learners. It integrates the latest ideas and research into a practical framework to create an inclusive reading curriculum and support learners across the whole education spectrum, including those with the most complex needs. Each chapter includes a mixture of research, strategies, and case study examples, demonstrating how reading supports both wellbeing and access to learning and – with stories – provides a versatile vehicle to build on vocabulary and expand our ability to think and learn about our place in the world.

Teaching Reading to All Learners Including Those with Complex Needs is essential reading for both new and experienced professionals, teachers and special educational needs and disabilities coordinators (SENDCos) looking to develop an inclusive reading curriculum and culture which will positively impact on the outcomes of all young people.

Sarah Moseley has over 30 years of knowledge and experience within special and mainstream education from teaching assistant to headteacher, as well as a solid research background. Her masters and PhD degrees were in special education and focused specifically on the teaching of reading and self-esteem. Sarah currently works as an independent educational consultant (www.drsarahmoseley.com), specialising in school improvement and raising outcomes for all learners. Her key areas for support focus on all aspects of special educational needs and disability (SEND), teaching and learning, inclusion, behaviour, and the development of literacy/communication.

nasen is a professional membership association that supports all those who work with or care for children and young people with special and additional educational needs. Members include SENCOs, school leaders, governors/trustees, teachers, teaching assistants, support workers, other educationalists, students and families.

nasen supports its members through policy documents, peer-reviewed academic journals, its membership magazine *nasen Connect*, publications, professional development courses, regional networks and newsletters. Its website contains more current information such as responses to government consultations.

nasen's published documents are held in very high regard both in the UK and internationally.

For a full list of titles see: https://www.routledge.com/nasen-spotlight/book-series/FULNASEN

Other titles published in association with the National Association for Special Educational Needs (nasen):

Curricula for Teaching Children and Young People with Severe or Profound and Multiple Learning Difficulties: Practical strategies for educational professionals
Peter Imray and Viv Hinchcliffe
2013/pb: 978-0-415-83847-4

Time to Talk: Implementing outstanding practice in speech, language and communication
Jean Gross
2013/pb: 978-0-415-63334-5

Promoting and Delivering School-to-School Support for Special Educational Needs: A practical guide for SENCOs
Rita Cheminais
2013/pb 978-0-415-63370-3

Dyslexia and Inclusion: Classroom Approaches for Assessment, Teaching and Learning, 2ed
Gavin Reid
2012/pb: 978-0-415-60758-2

The Equality Act for Educational Professionals: A simple guide to disability and inclusion in schools
Geraldine Hills
2012/pb: 978-0-415-68768-3

Using Playful Practice to Communicate with Special Children
Margaret Corke
2012/pb: 978-0-415-68767-6

Language for Learning in the Secondary School: A practical guide for supporting students with speech, language and communication needs
Sue Hayden and Emma Jordan
2012/pb: 978-0-415-61975-2

Providing Relationships and Sex Education for Special Learners: An Essential Guide for Developing RSE Provision
Paul Bray
2022/pb: 978-1-138-48747-5

Teaching Reading to All Learners Including Those with Complex Needs: A Framework for Progression within an Inclusive Reading Curriculum
Sarah Moseley
2023/pb: 978-1-032-11475-0

Teaching Reading to All Learners Including Those with Complex Needs
A Framework for Progression within an Inclusive Reading Curriculum

Sarah Moseley

LONDON AND NEW YORK

Designed cover image: © Getty Images

First published 2023
by Routledge
4 Park Square, Milton Park, Abingdon, Oxon OX14 4RN

and by Routledge
605 Third Avenue, New York, NY 10158

Routledge is an imprint of the Taylor & Francis Group, an informa business

© 2023 Sarah Moseley

The right of Sarah Moseley to be identified as author of this work has been asserted in accordance with sections 77 and 78 of the Copyright, Designs and Patents Act 1988.

All rights reserved. No part of this book may be reprinted or reproduced or utilised in any form or by any electronic, mechanical, or other means, now known or hereafter invented, including photocopying and recording, or in any information storage or retrieval system, without permission in writing from the publishers.

Trademark notice: Product or corporate names may be trademarks or registered trademarks, and are used only for identification and explanation without intent to infringe.

British Library Cataloguing-in-Publication Data
A catalogue record for this book is available from the British Library

ISBN: 978-1-032-11474-3 (hbk)
ISBN: 978-1-032-11475-0 (pbk)
ISBN: 978-1-003-22004-6 (ebk)

DOI: 10.4324/9781003220046

Typeset in Helvetica
by Apex CoVantage, LLC

Contents

	Introduction	1
1	Why prioritise reading for all?	7
2	Where to begin and the importance of high expectations	21
3	The importance of accessible literacy-rich environments	31
4	How does reading develop?	53
5	The role of foundation skills and the teaching of reading: where does phonics fit for learners with complex needs?	65
6	Why learners have difficulty learning to read: importance of the stages of processing and strategies to support	79
7	Practical ways into planning for an inclusive reading curriculum	87
	Conclusion	103
	Index	109

Introduction

This book has been a lifetime's thinking related to my own issues with reading and spelling, as well as my experiences working within mainstream and special education settings. Early on in my career, an Office for Standards in Education, Children's Services and Skills (Ofsted) inspector told me that I had the skills and passion to make a significant change to pupils' lives. I held onto that for many years, and nearly 15 years later, I became a headteacher. My journey took me through many different roles in education from teaching assistant to mainstream class teacher, senior leader within several special needs schools and headteacher of an all-ages special needs school.

My interest in research and developing a deeper understanding about how children and young people learn has led me to my current role working as an independent educational consultant. In this role, I have been fortunate enough to work with many professionals across different organisations, this has given me an even greater insight into how my experience, my research, and current thinking can be further developed in terms of creating an inclusive reading curriculum for all learners.

> **My experience**
>
> From the start of my career, I was aware that my passion lay in supporting those pupils in my classroom who had the most difficulties with literacy. When I qualified as a mainstream primary teacher, my first class of 32 Year 3 pupils was in an area of London where there was high social and economic deprivation. During my time teaching this group of children, I realised just how difficult it was for some children to learn to read. I wanted to support them as much as I could, and this interest led me to further studies and eventually a career within special education. This provided me with an opportunity to gain a real understanding about why learners struggle with literacy and with learning to read. Alongside the practitioner roles, I spent over 20 years as a researcher. I completed a master's degree and a PhD in special education, presented nationally/internationally at conferences, and became a published author of my research. I know that this passion and interest was fuelled by my own difficulties with literacy. I still struggle to spell a large number of words. I find reading new words and particularly names that I may have never come across difficult – and in many cases impossible. I have learnt coping mechanisms to support these issues, but I still have a moment of panic during my training sessions when I need to address someone by a name that I might not be able to say. I still feel the fear of getting it wrong and try to avoid situations where that might be the case.

Throughout my career, the one constant has been my belief in people and my belief that everyone can succeed in the right environment, with the right support and equal access to opportunities. This belief became my vision for education and later for my research into the teaching of reading to learners with complex needs. If there is one message that is central to this book, it is that we must as leaders believe that our pupils can achieve. At the heart of every organisation, there must be high expectations for the whole community. Leaders need to be aspirational for their pupils. In special education, this is highlighted further as pupils may need us to represent their wants, needs, and desires for them.

At the heart of my research over 15 years ago was a belief that every learner should have the opportunity to be taught to learn to read. The role of us as professionals is to consider how we can create accessible, engaging and motivating opportunities that are appropriate for the needs of all learners. This relates to our definition of literacy and the requirement of re-framing how we consider our literacy curriculum, and what this means for individual learners. During the writing

DOI: 10.4324/9781003220046-1

of this book, it became clear that what was missing was not more information about how we teach learners to read, but rather a pathway through this information that may help professionals, families, and learners with complex needs to understand what the issues may be and what barriers to learning may exist.

My writing has been influenced by the work of Erickson and Koppenhaver, who emphasise,

> *A book isn't a book, nor a pencil a pencil, if a student isn't able to use it. We need to adapt or create tools for literacy learning that students with physical impairments can hold, students with sensory impairments can see or hear, students with intellectual impairments can understand, and all students are motivated to use.*
>
> (Erickson & Koppenhaver, 2016)

Who is this book referring to?

Throughout the book, I will be using the term 'learners with complex needs' to refer to children and young people who may have severe to profound learning difficulties and disabilities (DfE, 2015).

Definitions of learning disabilities

The terms used to define learners with severe and profound learning difficulties are broad and have been interpreted differently by organisations and research. This has led to further confusion and difficulty for developing educational practise in this area.

- "Learning difficulties cover a wide range of needs, including moderate learning difficulties (MLD), severe learning difficulties (SLD), where children are likely to need support in all areas of the curriculum and associated difficulties with mobility and communication, through to profound and multiple learning difficulties (PMLD), where children are likely to have severe and complex learning difficulties as well as a physical disability or sensory impairment" (DfE, 2015).

    https://assets.publishing.service.gov.uk/government/uploads/system/uploads/attachment_data/file/398815/SEND_Code_of_Practice_January_2015.pdf

- "Lots of people with a profound and multiple learning disability can still be involved in decisions about themselves, do things they enjoy and be independent."

    www.nhs.uk/conditions/learning-disabilities/

Someone who has a severe learning disability will:

- have little or no speech
- find it very difficult to learn new skills
- need life-long support

    www.challengingbehaviour.org.uk/understanding-challenging-behaviour/what-is-challenging-behaviour/what-is-a-severe-learning-disability/

Instead, I used the term complex needs to include those children and young people who have a complex learning profile, in addition to a learning disability. They may also have other conditions that coexist and interconnect such as physical, sensory, communication, behavioural, or health needs.

The definition used is wide, as I want to develop our understanding of how children and young people learn to read and then look at the barriers that may exist. I am aiming to avoid any preconceived ideas that come with specific definitions, as these may act as barriers in themselves. It is important to remember that we are all unique, whether we have complex learning needs or not. This book is not about defining specific needs or abilities but rather aims to provide a greater understanding about how we can use existing knowledge and best practice to support learners across this spectrum of complex needs.

This book contains strategies and approaches that have worked in different contexts, or that are backed up by research. I have included practical real-life examples from practitioners working within special school settings within the UK, to support and illustrate some of the impact of strategies I am discussing.

> ### Ideas in action: case study from a special school
>
> **School** – Cate Hunter, Croftcroighn Primary School, Glasgow. Croftcroighn Primary School is a special school for learners with complex additional support needs, including cognitive, sensory, communication and physical impairments from P1–P7. The school has a nursery which admits children from the age of 2 years. There are currently 61 pupils at the school.
>
> **Context** – The group involved were seven learners with complex needs who range in ability from P3–P5.
>
> **Intent** – My focus was developing a reading culture and increased access to print for all.
>
> **Implementation** – Every child, regardless of age or ability, was given the opportunity to access the written word by choosing a book as part of a soft-start. Once the child had settled with a chosen book an adult interacted, by reading the story to them, and/or talking about the illustrations. Their interest in particular books were shared with their parents.
>
> Communication has been a focus, and I have given the children the opportunity to develop their love of stories through experiencing sensory stories. These include opportunities to act out parts of the story together, use different character voices, introduce a variety of props, and introduce symbols, and allowing the children to make decisions about some aspect of the story and encourage the children to interact and control the way the story is told.
>
> We focused on Picture Exchange Communication System (PECS) and Augmentative and Alternative Communication (AAC) incorporating low tech to high tech using simple letters, words, and picture boards linked to the story, asking repetitive questions over the literacy block, as well as introducing only one topic of conversation at a time. I have linked in rhymes that are very popular in class.
>
> I have focused on labelling the environment with corresponding large print, symbols, and text-rich displays. The library is always open, accessible, and inclusive.
>
> **Impact** – More time is now spent exploring books and text with increased engagement. When I ask a question, the waiting time and interaction time have reduced. Some children are now selecting PECS for rhymes with linked switch activities. Engagement and enjoyment have increased throughout.

Every learner contains a completely unique learning profile and set of strengths, weaknesses, and motivators. Learners with the most complex needs will have an even greater uniqueness surrounding this learning profile, due to their learning difficulties, experiences, and the opportunities that have been presented to them. An important finding of my own research was that in many cases, learners with complex needs have not been provided with consistent opportunities to be taught the mechanics of learning to read. There are many reasons why this may be the case, from a lack of appropriate professional development to the understanding of how to teach reading to learners with complex needs and why this is important.

One of the reasons for writing this book is the many conversations that I have had with professionals working within special education who have asked me to support the implementation of a more inclusive approach to the teaching of literacy – specifically reading – across their schools. I will discuss reasons why the teaching of reading has gained a greater presence within the special school curriculum, and how this has led to further uncertainty. There are mixed feelings amongst professionals, academics, and researchers – as well as families – about the appropriateness and applicability of the teaching of literacy – specifically reading – to all learners. In my experience, I have found that the implementation of previous government led strategies have made many people wary. For example, the National Literacy Strategy led to some blanket expectations and experiences for learners within special school classrooms where mainstream practice was expected to be replicated (Lacey et al., 2007). All learners were included within the traditional structure of the literacy hour, within the National Literacy Strategy unless there was clear evidence that a different approach was needed. This led to many practices which were deemed as inappropriate for learners with complex needs.

The inclusion of learners into a structure where they may have been passive participants of an activity that happened around them and to them, rather than with them, has led to a divide in thinking between special education and mainstream education.

In this book, I will address some of these issues and ensure that what is proposed and discussed is something that puts engagement and participation of learners at the heart. The crucial role that personalisation of experiences and opportunities play, alongside elements of choice and accessible experiences, is key. What is certain is that we do not know what any learner is capable of, and this includes those with complex needs. Although this is the case in some contexts, learners are labelled from an early age as non-readers within special education, unable to access something that we are all immersed in. This can lead to a lack of expectations for our learners with complex needs and a narrowing of the curriculum. If we believe they cannot, then we will not provide the opportunities – and this therefore becomes a self-fulling prophesy (Rosenthal & Jacobson 1968).

My experience

I have written this book after many years of experience and research, and although I do appreciate that this is a view that may not be accepted by others, I am clear that it is us as professionals who need to reconsider how we define what literacy is for learners and the impact this has on what we provide in terms of our curriculum. If we change how we define literacy and widen it to be a more inclusive view, then we can create a more inclusive curriculum whereby learners with complex needs are part of this. When we consider reading in terms of a more inclusive definition, it enables us to ensure that we are providing opportunities for every learner to access this framework. If we decide that learners with the most complex needs are not readers, due to a narrow definition, we are excluding a whole group of learners from a framework that is at the heart of education. If we consider reading to be accessing literacy, developing an awareness of sound and the ability to listen, thus accessing meaning from some form of stimuli, we can then open an inclusive reading framework as part of what already exists. We can then talk about the pathways learners are on, and the way that they are readers and develop confidence amongst us all in terms of sharing literacy experiences and interactions. Unless we expect learners to participate in their own way, and give them the opportunity to participate, then they will not be able to do it. Koppenhaver and Erickson (2020) emphasise that progress begins when learning opportunity begins.

We should see the learners we work with as readers and writers in the widest sense – we need to have an expectation that the teaching of reading has an important role within their education and life. This is true for communication, as we would not label a learner as a non-communicator at an early age. Instead, we would work with them to develop and support a system that enables participation and expression in a way that is appropriate for them. I recently read a quote on the Talk Sense website that used the analogy of winning the lottery when referring to the importance of teaching emergent literacy skills. The quote stated,

> *If we never make any attempt, by definition, a person has no chance of gaining such skills. How do you win the lottery? You purchase a ticket! Sure there is a remote chance but if you never purchase a ticket, you definitely will not win.*
>
> (Talk Sense, 2022)

Why focus on reading

Research historically emphasised that reading is key to education, and education the key to success in our society (Adams, 1990; Snowling & Hume, 2006). The importance of teaching all young people to read has gained significance over the last 30 years, as there has been a growth in research-based practice. This is due to the positive impact – both emotionally and academically – it has for the education of all young people. As summed up by Such (2021, p. 1), "few impediments undermine a person's aspirations as effectively as an inability to read".

Research promotes reading as the key to closing the gap for all learners (Education Endowment Foundation, 2020). For our learners with identified special educational needs and disability (SEND), the role of reading has an even greater significance. Reading can provide a window into a wider world that we can all enter, regardless of our ability! It is established that learning to read has a powerful role in increasing engagement and motivation, aspects that are particularly important for all learners with complex needs. Significantly, reading can provide independence and freedom, building on our vocabulary and expanding our ability to think and learn about our place in the world. If we get it right, we give children access to a world of learning and a never-ending source of pleasure and knowledge about themselves and the world around them. Being part of a literacy rich reading culture can only enhance and add to the lives of all learners. Learners will have opportunities to experience and develop a wider vocabulary, as well as knowledge of the world, and others. There will be opportunities for increased engagement and attention span, supporting learners to focus and attend, manipulating their bodies for meaningful reasons. This leads to an increased awareness of print, something that surrounds us all – no matter what our abilities are. This needs to be understood and implemented in a way that celebrates and supports accessibility of literacy for all learners. To ensure that engagement, participation and choice are at the heart of any inclusive reading framework.

The real-life examples of learners with complex needs that I have included demonstrate the impact of providing a rich literacy environment, alongside structured opportunities to develop an understanding of literacy. These include an impact on learners' speech and language development, increased engagement and participation within the classroom, improved self-esteem, a reduction in challenging behaviour and increased ability to attend to activities across the curriculum. My own research found that changes in self-esteem and confidence were noted within the classroom and home environment (Moseley, 2005, 2009, 2015). Each chapter will aim to provide some strategies to ensure this important two-way relationship is promoted and valued across an inclusive reading framework.

Aims of the book

This book aims to bridge the gap between theory and practice to provide professionals and families with the knowledge and confidence to develop reading for all learners. I aim to use what is known about good practice in teaching reading and how reading develops to support the development of an inclusive reading curriculum for all.

Finally, a word of caution: This book does not attempt to answer all the questions or promote one specific viewpoint. Its foundation is based on my experience of working with learners with complex needs, my research focusing on teaching reading to these learners, and my experience of working with over 300 professionals through my training and consultancy. As such, its aim is to add to the body of information in the field and provide professionals and families with the knowledge to make their own decisions. I truly feel that knowledge is power and it is only through a clarity of the knowledge that is out there that individuals have the power to make decisions that support the best outcomes for all children and young people.

Organisation of the book

Each of the chapters is structured around a summary of theories within specific areas, alongside real-life examples of ideas in action. This is followed by discussion of how this may present with each learner and finally points for reflection and further reading. This book aims to clearly set out the core principles for teaching all children to read, to enable everyone to be included in the wonderful world of literature and access education to their full potential. I present my personal views and experiences of being a teacher, leader, and researcher during a period of rapid change in expectations and how we judge achievement for learners with complex needs. My aim is to provide the information needed, based on a greater understanding of the impact that developing an understanding of literacy will have for all learners, including those with complex needs.

> **Time to think**
>
> What three things would you like to learn after reading this book?
> Make a note of these, and if they are not answered, please get in touch!
>
> www.drsarahmoseley.com
> Facebook, Instagram, LinkedIn: Dr Sarah Moseley
> Twitter: @drsarahmoseley

References

Adams, M.J. (1990) *Beginning to Read: Thinking and Learning about Print*. Cambridge: MA: MIT Press.

DfE (2015) *Special educational needs and disability code of practice: 0 to 25 years statutory guidance for organisations which work with and support children and young people who have special educational needs or disabilities* Available at: https://assets.publishing.service.gov.uk/government/uploads/system/uploads/attachment_data/file/398815/SEND_Code_of_Practice_January_2015.pdf [Accessed: 14/06/2022]

Education Endowment Foundation. (2020) *Literacy: Improving the teaching and learning of literacy* [online] Available at: https://educationendowmentfoundation.org.uk/guidance-for-teachers/literacy [Accessed: 14/06/2022]

Erickson, K. & Koppenhaver, D. (2016) *Literacy instruction for students with significant disabilities* [online] Available at: https://literacyforallinstruction.ca/access-to-books/#:~:text=%E2%80%9CA%20book%20isn%E2%80%99t%20a%20book%2C%20nor%20a%20pencil,understand%2C%20and%20all%20students%20are%20motivated%20to%20use.%E2%80%9D [Accessed: 12/06/2022]

Koppenhaver, D. & Erickson, K. (2020) *Comprehensive Literacy for All: Teaching Students with Significant Disabilities to Read and Write*. Baltimore, MD, London, Sydney: Paul H. Brookes Publishing Co.

Lacey, P., Layton, L., Miller, C., Goldbart, J. & Lawson, H. (2007) What is literacy for students with severe learning difficulties? Exploring conventional and inclusive literacy. *Journal of Research in Special educational Needs*, 7, (3), pp. 149–160 [online] Available at: https://citeseerx.ist.psu.edu/viewdoc/download?doi=10.1.1.672.2404&rep=rep1&type=pdf [Accessed: 30/06/2022]

Moseley, S. (2005) *Developing a measure of self-concept for children and young people with severe learning difficulties*. The SLD Experience, Spring.

Moseley, S. (2009) *The effect of reading instruction on the self-concept and self-esteem of pupils with severe learning disabilities*. Ph.D. Thesis. University of London Institute of Education, London.

Moseley, S. (2015) The teaching of reading to learners with SLD. In P. Lacey, R. Ashdown, P. Jones, H. Lawson & M. Pipe (Eds.) *The Routledge Companion to Severe, Profound and Multiple Learning Difficulties*. London: Routledge.

Rosenthal, R. & Jacobson, L. (1968) Pygmalion in the classroom. *The Urban Review*, 3, pp. 16–20 Available at: www.semanticscholar.org/paper/Pygmalion-in-the-classroom-Rosenthal-Jacobson/59c14fab51544dc9c5ec4e56c5a962346859c06a#paper-header [Accessed: 29/06/2022]

Snowling, M. & Hume, C. (2006) Language skills, learning to read and reading intervention. *London Review of Education*, 4, (1), pp. 63–76 Available at: www.scienceopen.com/document_file/e2b57a2e-d408-4e00-8b38-ce1596047874/ScienceOpen/s6.pdf [Accessed: 18/06/2022]

Such, C. (2021) *The Art and Science of Teaching Primary Reading*. London: SAGE Publications Ltd.

Talk Sense. (2022) *101 ideas for literacy & AAC* [online] Available at: https://talksense.weebly.com/literacy-and-aac.html [Accessed: 19/06/2022]

1 Why prioritise reading for all?

In this chapter, the focus will be on the importance of reading for all learners. The positive impact that reading has on how we feel – especially how we feel about ourselves as learners – will be discussed. The role that reading plays in promoting independence and increased autonomy for learners with complex needs will be emphasised. At the heart of this will be the understanding that good practice in the teaching of reading is good for all learners, including those with complex needs.

There has been a large body of research focusing on the importance of reading to young children and the impact on later academic ability. Research emphasises that learning to read accurately by the age of 6 enables a child to learn to read for the rest of their life. Reading failure begins early and has a long-term impact (DfE, 2021). There is clear evidence that learning to read in fact has a long-term impact on learners' later success within society. Research evidence discussed within the reading framework (DfE, 2021) from the Organisation for Economic Co-operation and Development's (OECD) Programme for International Student Assessment (PISA) advocates that in fact, "finding ways to engage students in reading may be one of the most effective ways to leverage social change" (OECD, 2002). This is powerful. Reading and learning to read has the capacity to create a huge change within society. The question that is then posed is: How does this relate to the teaching of reading to learners with complex needs?

Research has established the significant positive impact that the teaching of reading has on the education of all young people. The Education Endowment Foundation emphasises reading as the key to closing the gap for learners following the COVID-19 pandemic (Civinini, 2020). Reading enables us to develop cognitively and expand our understanding of ourselves and the world around us; we can go to places and times we never imagined. Reading enables us to be independent, leading to increased freedom. Reading is established as having a positive impact on how we feel (Clark & Picton, 2020), especially how we feel about ourselves as learners. In a climate where the importance of mental health is high on the agenda, reading is seen as a priority for all.

For our learners with complex needs, the role of reading has an even greater significance. The environments and experiences of all learners have been reduced due to the pandemic, and for those with the most complex needs, this impact is huge.

- Reading provides a window into a wider world that we can all enter, regardless of our ability.
- Reading a story requires extraordinarily little to begin – just us, imagination, enthusiasm, and aspirations for our learners.
- Yet there is a lack of clarity around teaching reading to learners with complex needs, and this does not support an inclusive education system for all learners.

> ### Ideas in action: case study from a family
>
> **Context** – After one of my training sessions, I was contacted by Alison, whose son's life had been enriched through the power of stories and sharing in reading activities. Alison had emailed me to tell me about her son, who from an early age had been diagnosed with complex profound multiple learning difficulties.
>
> **Intent** – As an early years practitioner, Alison had started to share and read books to her son Timmy at 2½ as a way to try to hold his attention and as a bridge to work with him.
>
> **Implementation** – His early collection included some of the classic stories such as *The Very Hungry Caterpillar* and *Hairy McClary*. Timmy's collection grew and at the start of his reading journey he appeared to understand a small range of symbol cards, after having related them to books, and these became a lifeline later in life when he became very ill.
>
> Timmy liked to listen to stories, and audio books were a favourite. Later in life, Timmy became very unwell but books enabled him to have a structure and scaffold for people to spend time and enjoy his company (Figure 1.1); they became a bridge for people to relate

to him. The family would create personalised books for Timmy, which he really enjoyed spending time looking at. By the age of 16, anything exciting would cause great pain and agitation for Timmy. For his 17th birthday, he had a drop-in day with friends; each of them called in to read a book to him. The Dreams Come True charity organised for Timmy to be read to by Julia Donaldson (Figure 1.2). This face-to-face event during Timmy's illness was a wonderful day for him. She read him his favourite book and gave us all sorts of treasured delights. Alison shared the poignant part of Timmy's life, that when he died at the age of 20 he took a number of his favourite books with him tucked into his coffin.

Impact – Timmy's mum Alison strongly felt that "investing in reading at a young age gave . . . a life of joy and pleasure". Timmy was able to recognise and engage with over 300 picture books and had a passion for and love of books, despite such limited understanding.

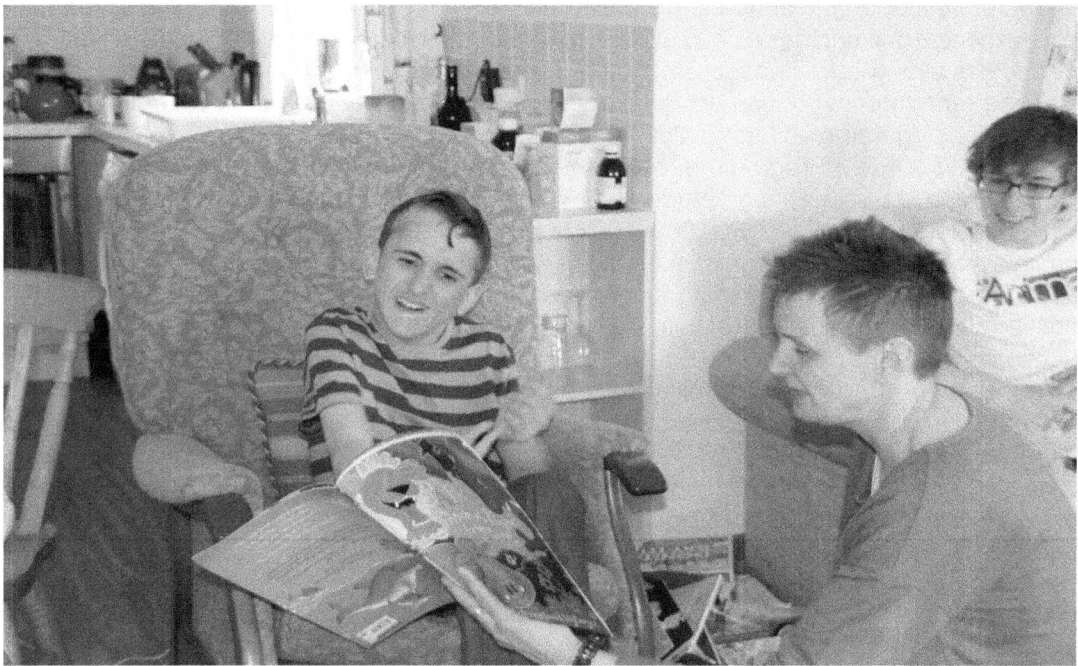

Figure 1.1 Timmy enjoying some of his favourite books.

Figure 1.2 Timmy being read one of his favourite books by Julia Donaldson facilitated by the Dreams Come True charity.

Why is learning to read so important?

Reading is emphasised to be the gateway to learning for typically developing learners. It can open doors for enjoyment and academic success, through enabling learners to gain information for themselves. Learning to read alongside having a broad and rich exposure to literature is important to provide opportunities for pupils to experience the wider world and enrich the curriculum for all. There are many reasons why reading is an important part of all our lives, from:

- Providing an inclusive gateway for all to access that can take learners outside of their current setting or situation
- Reading to learn something new, to obtain information that will help make choices and decisions
- Reading to make us think about things in a new or different way
- Helping us to understand others and develop empathy, building our relationships and increasing our concentration
- Reading for pleasure and to be entertained; for example, providing opportunities to experience the lives of others in different times, places, and cultures
- Reading to be inspired and provide access to the wider world
- Reading to keep us informed
- Reading to help us understand others better. It enables us to develop cognitively and expand our understanding of ourselves and the world around us – we can go to places and times we never imagined
- Reading to help us understand ourselves better
- Importantly it builds on our vocabulary and expands our ability to think and learn

Research is clear that reading supports us to feel good about ourselves; we all need to be a part of this reading community that we see others accessing every day (Krishnan & Johnson, 2014). Research has demonstrated that reading aloud creates a sense of community, building a shared reading history and community (Cremin et al., 2014). Print is everywhere, as are people reading and talking about literacy/books. It is part of our world, regardless of our ability to access it. If we do not include the existence of print or text within all learning experiences, we are ignoring part of our children and young people's environment that is key for everyone else. We talk about reading in many senses, e.g., reading situations or peoples faces. Yet we have a restrictive definition when we talk about all learners reading. Being provided with specific reading opportunities provides expectations that they are part of this world.

Reading therefore provides us with many different things as well as making us feel good about ourselves as learners. In a world of uncertainty, it can provide a known experience, a consistency that we can all share for our learners. In her influential work in this area, Flo Longhorn emphasises the importance of literacy as providing ways in for all learners in terms of their emotions, communication, and expressing themselves through literacy (Longhorn, 2001).

My own experiences

Personally, I found my schooling experience enjoyable – but at times, I struggled. Specifically, learning to spell and reading aloud filled me with fear. I would often avoid activities where either of these was required; my approach was to remain very quiet at the back of the class. Unfortunately for me, I have always been a tall person and even at 11 years of age had to stand at the back with the boys during school photos due to my height!

If we all try to remember our days in the classroom, I am sure that few specific experiences are vivid. For me, two key reading aloud experiences stand out. The first was being asked to read whilst standing up in front of the class as a 8-year-old when I was so scared. Later I recall at the age of 11 standing up in assembly, reading out my project and being presented with a commemorative coin from the Tower of London. The difference in those two experiences related to the meaningfulness of the context. The second situation involved me reading something I had written and produced based on a topic I loved. I

> have a passion for the Tudor period and the project focused on the Tower of London and Henry VIII. I just loved the image of the Tudor rose.
>
> I had won the award for the best project (I am sure there were more criteria than simply best, but that is what I remember!). Even today I am continually inspired and interested in anything associated with this period in history, from teaching it to my own classes, to reading fiction set during this time, to planning a visit to Hampton Court with my young son. If I had never had the opportunity to experience and learn about the Tudors, I would have missed out on the enjoyment and support that this has provided me. History gave me the motivation to learn more, the confidence to speak/read in front of others, and an interest in a whole new genre of books.
>
> Historically, there has been a lack of professional development to support those who work with learners with complex needs, specifically those who work within special education. In recent years, initial teacher training has begun to catch up and there is a greater availability of courses, modules, and practical advice around what works for learners with complex needs. In many contexts this is optional, and once you secure a post within special education, the continued professional development (CPD) available may be limited. There is a growing awareness that the context of all schools is changing, in many cases the number of learners accessing mainstream education who have a higher level of special educational needs is increasing.

Historically, the trend towards inclusion of all children into a mainstream environment resulted in a change in the populations of all schools (Imray, 2007). The move for greater inclusion has, in many cases, led to the increasing educational placement of more able pupils with special educational needs and disabilities into mainstream (Male & Rayner, 2007). The publication of the SEND Green Paper (DfE, 2022) has once more placed inclusion high on the educational agenda. There is a clear drive to ensure that all local authorities and mainstream schools develop more inclusive practices, "Changing the culture and practice in mainstream education to be more inclusive and better at identifying and supporting needs, including through earlier intervention and improved targeted support" (DfE, 2022).

The Green Paper calls for an improvement in the transparency of provision provided for learners with SEND, including the creation of inclusive plans and dashboards. Local authorities will need to illustrate steps that are taken to ensure that all learners are able to achieve, regardless of the school that they attend. The implication of this is that professionals need to be skilled in creating opportunities for all learners to achieve and reach their potential. This will increase the need for a more inclusive definition of reading to be used across education, enabling the curriculum to be looked at in a different way. The focus needs to be on how we can remove barriers to learning for all children and young people, as opposed to them fitting into an existing understanding of what they need to do to become a reader.

Current thinking

It is important to briefly discuss external pressures on special schools and why a shift in thinking has been further prompted in terms of the teaching of reading. The Ofsted Education Inspection Framework (EIF; Ofsted, 2019) placed a renewed focus on the teaching of reading, specifically early reading. As Ofsted summed up, "It is almost impossible to overestimate the importance of literacy . . . . Literacy is empowering it gives children independence to explore what interests them." (Ofsted, 2019)

Ofsted's Education Inspection Framework also placed a greater emphasis on the development of vocabulary as the key to expanding a young person's mind, language, and thinking about the world. Vocabulary is expanded by exposing children and young people to a wider range of subjects and experiences, specifically through books and exposure to rich literacy environments. This is important for all learners. As emphasised in the reading framework, "Evidence indicates that the number of words heard by young children by the time they are five is increased from 4,662 (if never read to) to 296,660 (if read to daily)" (Science Daily, 2019).

All schools will be subject to a reading deep dive, where the focus on how all learners are taught to read. The term 'deep dive' is used to refer to Ofsted focusing on the teaching of reading as a key line of inquiry. The deep dive investigates how the reading curriculum is designed, looking at what is trying to be achieved, the sequence of progression, the strengths and weaknesses of the curriculum, and so forth. We all need to be clear of the reading curriculum provided for our pupils – specifically the intent, implementation, and impact of our reading methodology.

> ### The 3 I's in terms of reading
>
> **Intent** – How determined schools are that all pupils will have the opportunities to develop core skills, regardless of ability. The headteacher and senior leaders ensure that the teaching of reading is given priority and emphasis across the school with clarity of approach for learners with more complex needs.
>
> **Implementation** – This is you! To be successful, there needs to be a shared clarity and understanding of how pupils learn to read. The assessment of pupils' ability and progress should be a regular informative activity embedded into practice.
>
> **Impact** – This means that all pupils, including the weakest readers, make sufficient progress appropriate to their level, and that pupils are familiar with and enjoy listening to a wide range of stories, poems, rhymes, and non-fiction (Ofsted, 2019).

The 3 I's have created much anxiety and fear amongst education professionals; what is required is termed as a 'strong response'. That is the ability to be clear about where a pupil is and where they are going; this is true for all pupils. It is about how we ensure pupils are supported with the skills to access, make progress, and ultimately enjoy reading (in its widest term) being immersed in a wide-ranging literacy world.

This framework is applied to all schools, requiring a clear strategy to be in place that ensures opportunities for every learner to become a reader. The emphasis in the framework is on how well pupils are taught to read, specifically how schools reach the lowest-attaining pupils. This has placed a greater emphasis on the role of reading within the curriculum across all special schools. If a school was inspected under the current education framework, it would need to have a response that was clear and concise around what provision was in place for learners in all areas of the school. This response needs to be consistent across the school, based on evidence of outcomes, and impact of current practice for all learners.

The positive implication of this is that the teaching of reading is on the agenda for all learners, regardless of their ability. The flip side of this is that there are no clear answers to support how this will then look for those learners who do not fit into a specific model or approach. The reading framework (DfE, 2021) promotes the importance of the teaching of reading to all learners; this includes learners with complex needs. This has created an increased emphasis on reading for all schools but a lack of clarity around how this is to be applied and what this means for learners with SEND and the most complex learning needs.

Changes faced by special schools

Special education has faced a continued period of rapid and complex change in terms of expectations for all pupils, from the inclusion of all pupils into the national curriculum (DfE, 2014), creation of 'P scales' (attainment targets for pupils with SEN) – for pupils below age-related expectations, the replacement of these by the engagement model (gov.uk, 2021) and changes in Ofsted's Education Inspection Framework (2019) with its emphasis on the teaching of reading. All these changes to policy, expectations, and culture have occurred in an environment where a lack of research and information has been available for leaders.

Changes to mainstream education have historically been applied to special school settings with very little guidance or research to support them. This has left special schools with a lack of confidence in many of the mainstream-based approaches that then require a huge amount of work to make them appropriate and applicable for learners with complex needs. For example, the reading framework discusses the importance of fidelity to one structured synthetic phonics approach. This recommendation has led to some concern across special school settings. In my role as a trainer and consultant, I have supported many professionals and schools with this specific issue.

The recommendation assumes that:

1. That there is a structured approach to the teaching of reading within the school
2. That there is a structured approach to the teaching of phonics
3. That the teaching of phonics is carried out using one approach

> **Reading framework: teaching the foundations of literacy (DfE, 2021)**
>
> - Provides specific guidance around good practice for all learners, including those with severe SEND and complex needs
> - Explicitly states that literacy should be taught to all learners with high expectation and ambition
> - Focuses on importance of systematic synthetic phonics (SSP)

The recommendation does not say that schools must select a validated scheme, but it does state that whichever approach is used, there needs to be robust and reliable evidence of its effectiveness and impact. The concern is that no one approach or scheme for any aspect of the curriculum for learners with complex needs is – on its own – appropriate for all learners. The notion of one size fitting all is certainly not the case when it comes to learners who have complex learning profiles. We will discuss this in more detail in the following chapters.

The curriculum for learners with the most complex needs has undergone a great deal of change since the introduction of the national curriculum. There has been an increase in research, practice, and discussion around what works for learners with complex needs, specifically those with the most profound complex needs. The importance of a more personalised, sensory curriculum is the foundation of the framework offered by most special schools for their learners at the earliest stages of development.

This is often referred to as the pre-formal curriculum. The pre-formal curriculum relates to the opportunities and experiences offered to learners who are at the earliest stage of cognitive development. The curriculum generally focuses on the key aspects of communication, engagement, interaction, and participation. The focus often is not subject specific, instead emphasising a curriculum designed to support all learners to develop and progress in terms of their social, emotional, and physical development. The key drivers tend to focus on engagement, communication, and independence. An example of the elements that may make up a pre-formal curriculum for learners follows.

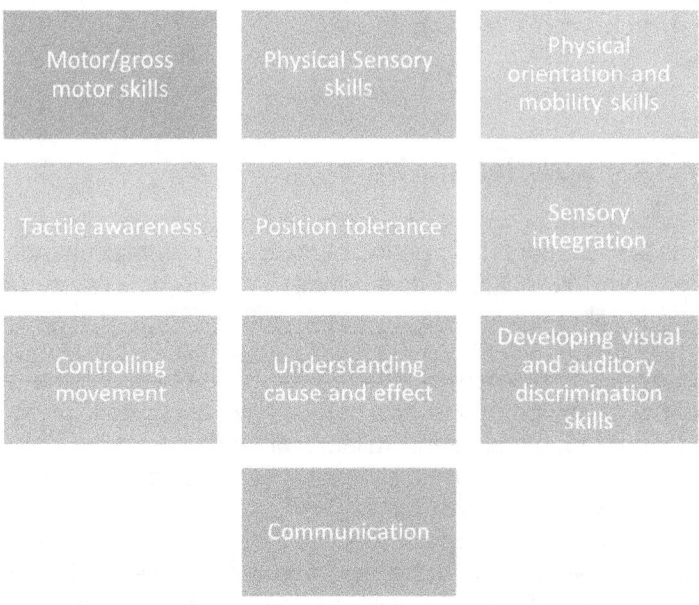

Figure 1.3 Elements of a pre-formal curriculum.

> **Ideas in action: curriculum pathways at a special school**
>
> **Context** – Fairfields School Northampton is a primary special school for children between the ages of 4 and 11 with severe or profound learning, communication, and physical difficulties. We also cater for pupils on the autistic spectrum. Some children may also have multi-sensory impairment and complex medical needs. There are currently 125 pupils on roll.
>
> **Intent** – Our curriculum is designed to provide opportunities for pupils to develop the skills, knowledge, and understanding that will enable them to have learning for life. Our curriculum builds on the foundations of previous learning, with a balance between the academic, personal development and enrichment.
>
> **Implementation** – The national curriculum subjects are taught through a thematic approach, enriched by literature, to ensure that pupils get this broad range of experiences and learning opportunities. The curriculum content in each subject has been selected for its relevance for our pupils' developmental level.
>
> Lesley Elder, headteacher, Fairfields

The engagement model

The process used to monitor progress for learners with complex needs has moved away from P levels and best fit to the use of an engagement model. The introduction of the engagement model places the focus back on the learner and provides us with information about how learners engage at this earliest level of development, as Penny Lacey emphasised,

> *I can't just give sensory experiences and hope that learning will take place. I need to know how many times to repeat the stimulus, what the likely reaction will be, how long it takes for that reaction to occur, where the best reactions take place.*
>
> (Lacey, 2001, p. 46)

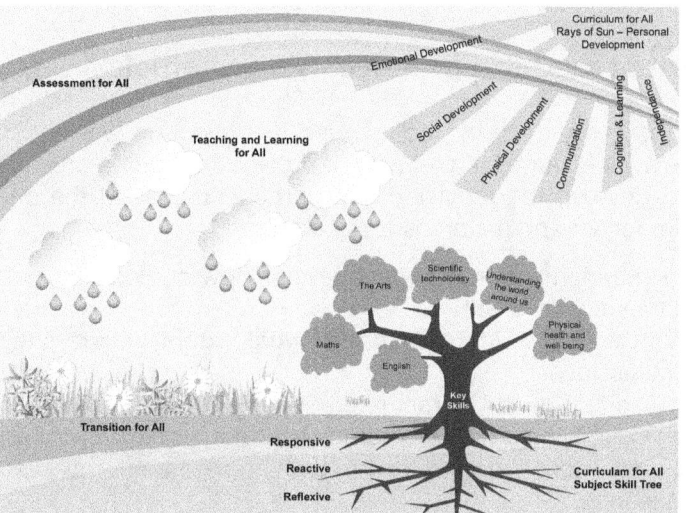

Assessment for All is designed to ensure we are measuring the small steps of progress each pupil makes, reflecting their own learning journey. Within the essential learning areas we assess progress of communication, whilst reading and phonics falls within the core learning areas.	**The Fairfields 'For All' Framework**	Our Curriculum for All provides specific developmental objectives for a pupil which means they can access their learning at an appropriate level to make progress across the curriculum. The 'Rays of Sun' covers areas related to personal development and the tree focuses on the subject skills. Communication sits within the 'Rays of Sun' and links closely to the child's EHC Plan. Reading and phonics sits within the English branch of the curriculum tree. Knowledge maps help sequence the skills and are matched to the bands of our assessment document.
Teaching and Learning for All provides details of the different approaches used across the curriculum to ensure effective teaching and learning. We use a variety of approaches to enhance reading and phonics across the school including Talk for Writing and Read Write Inc.	Transition for all occurs at the start of the academic year, allowing teachers to spend quality time to observe the children and get to know them, finding out their motivators and interests. This time also allows teachers to layer in structure and routine whilst building relationships. From this reflective practice, they can create an environment which meets the children's needs.	

https://fairfields.northants.sch.uk/

Figure 1.4 Adapted from Fairfields School's 'For All' Framework.

14 *Why prioritise reading for all?*

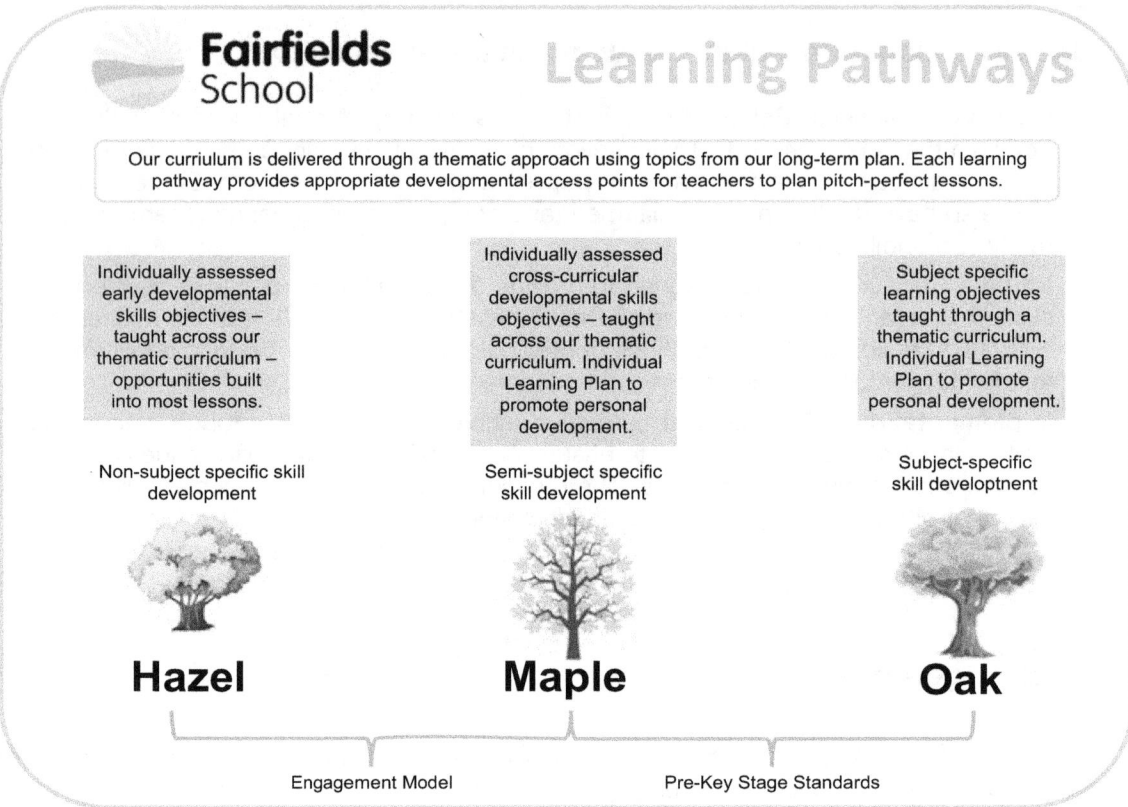

Figure 1.5 Adapted from Fairfields School's Learning Pathways to guide teachers with the use of the curriculum. This helps ensure pupils' learning is personalised and that the learning is appropriate to the pupils' developmental level.

The model builds on the strengths of the learner, through observations and recording of responses to stimuli, situations, and environments. It provides a way of building up a profile of engagement in relation to experiences and opportunities they are part of.

The engagement model in practice: Nick Sheffield

The model informs every decision, adjustment, or reflection we make in the pre-formal curriculum pathway. It is our eyes and ears; it provides us with a crucial pupil voice which helps shape and develop the provision and curriculum around the child. We follow the model of observe, reflect and action as a key mantra.

- We create an engagement profile which tells us how our learners gather and use information from their environment.
- We then have the tool which monitors to what extent we are seeing these learning behaviours in sessions.
- We then respond to how the learner interacts to increase engagement in their environment and curriculum, which in turn promotes attainment and success for the individual.
- This provides information around how to gain engagement, participation, and motivation from the learner.

Is literacy part of the curriculum framework?

In many pre-formal curriculum frameworks, literacy is included. It is acknowledged that literacy provides learners with the opportunity to experience and to gain a greater understanding of the world around them. For some learners on a pre-formal pathway, literacy – and specifically reading – is not part of the curriculum offer, or a key aspect of this environment. The Equals

Pre-formal curriculum has been designed for a small percentage of the population who are working at significantly below the age-related peers for all their adult lives, and literacy is not a specific strand (Imray, 2021). Many pre-formal curriculum-based models are project focused, whereby learners are taught through interest and engagement as opposed to a predefined set of national curriculum objectives (Imray, 2021). The emphasis is said to be on strengthening and deepening knowledge, rather than catching up, the implication being that these are opposing rather than similar views with a difference in emphasis. As discussed earlier, incorporating an inclusive reading framework is not a case of either/or, but as well as. There is no focus on catching up, but the same focus on deepening understanding.

In a framework whereby literary and specifically reading is not referenced, there may not be any suggestions on how it may be incorporated, or how a learner's understanding or awareness of this can be supported. The question that I pose is: How do we enrich approaches and strategies based on good practice of the effectiveness of multi-sensory learning with our understanding of emergent literacy development? We know that our senses are key to learning across all areas of the curriculum, and therefore let us enrich our offer for all learners. As Flo Longhorn (2001) emphasises, we must ensure all learners have the opportunity to be part of a rich literacy curriculum.

If the view is held that one specific approach is better than another, this can lead to the exclusion of existing practice which is established as fundamental to specific aspects of learning, in this case the teaching of reading.

Information gathering and information sharing at the heart of engagement

All learning and interactions start by taking information out of our environment by exploring through our senses. We do this all of the time – sometimes purposefully, sometimes not. We then use this information to inform our actions on our environment. These actions should result in our immediate environment changing and evolving around the learner. This is how our learners become impactful and active members of their classrooms. Whether or not we continue to engage, whether we change the way we explore, have we started to anticipate what happens next? Do we ask for more? Do we reject it? We should not differentiate learning opportunities, but we should provide different learning opportunities for all. We do not do differentiation; we do different.

Research focusing on the importance of teachers having a positive approach to the learning process concludes that unless there is an expectation that pupils can learn, they will not be provided with opportunities to try (Kasa-Hendrickson, 2005). The publication of the reading framework (DfE, 2021) included clear discussion around learners with complex needs. It explicitly states that literacy should be taught to all learners with high expectation and ambition. There has been discussion about the types of learners they were referring to and the appropriateness of some of the strategies discussed, as well as the research that these recommendations were based upon. What is clear is that we need to find a way through the differences that exist across academia, education, and government guidance to ensure we promote the best outcomes for all learners.

Nick Sheffield

Ideas in action: case study from a special school

Context – I am currently teaching a foundation phase complex needs class of seven students aged 4–11 within a special school. I previously taught for a year the secondary phase complex needs class of six students aged 11–19. Although literacy has always been a focus within the curriculum, accessing physical books and phonics for these learners has been limited and centred more around simple sensory activities.

Intent – To develop a language and literacy rich environment for all learners.

Implementation – This has led to the inclusion of not only more words in displays and around the classroom, but also the inclusion of Makaton signs to reinforce the language used incidentally throughout the day. We have started to use physical copies of the stories alongside the sensory story and have found that the students are focusing on the images and starting to anticipate turning the page, etc.

> **Impact** – Reading and exploring physical books including touch and feel, flaps, and interactive stories has also been introduced daily into the morning routine, which has had a massive impact on the interest in reading with all students. Some students are demonstrating an awareness of repeated stories and anticipating certain aspects, whilst others are showing more focus on the images and awareness of the book itself, even if it is a fleeting glance. Interactive stories have also been trialled and shown to be a big success with our students. An example of this is Tom Fletcher's *There's a Dragon in Your Book*. Each student had a copy to complete (with support) the interactive elements – e.g., stoking the dragon's nose – but sensory stimuli were used throughout, also. All students were engaged throughout, and showed positive reactions to physically interacting with the images and pages.
>
> Bethan Davies

The premise of this book is that we all need to be aware of what works in terms of the learning process for all learners, including those with complex needs. Therefore, providing all professionals with a tool bag of strategies that they can pull, which includes multi-sensory approaches alongside repetitive, engaging, and rich structured teaching. This is specifically important for learners with complex needs. High on the educational agenda has been the importance of research-based practice alongside an increased understanding about neurological processes, how we learn, how we think, and how we can support all learners with their progress. The future requires joined-up thinking that involves all professionals, families, and learners, focused on an understanding of learning styles and barriers to learning that may exist, combined with the importance of clear purposeful learning opportunities and experiences.

The view that I advocate within this book is based on my published empirical research findings as part of my PhD studies, articles, presentations at conferences internationally, experience in the classroom, leadership of literacy across special schools, and my consultancy work with many schools across the UK.

> ## My research
>
> My research focused on a small sample (45) of learners aged 11–13, in six different schools across the UK and Channel Islands (Moseley, 2009). The findings of my research were positive. All learners with complex needs made gains in their literacy development using a structured approach. It also affected the view that they held about themselves as learners, and as readers.
>
> I found conducting research in this area extremely challenging, for many reasons outside of the learner's control. The barriers were the following.
>
> 1. **Sample size** – Ensuring that I had a large enough sample, to be representative and allow for a control group to be used. Gaining the consent of participants within special schools was time consuming and difficult. The number of specialist provisions across the UK is far less than that of mainstream schools. Each of the schools is also different in terms of catchment area, and makeup of the needs of learners within each of the classes. Once schools had agreed to take part in the research, there was the issue of gaining the consent of learners, many of whom were non-verbal or had limited verbal ability.
> 2. **Workload concerns** – The complexity and uniqueness of the special school environment require continual adaptations of the curriculum, timetable, and general school life to meet the needs of all learners. The schools often have a high staff-to-pupil ratio, which means that staffing issues, absence management, training, communication, and systems take up large amounts of time. This fact, alongside the uniqueness and challenges of the role for professionals working with such a varied and diverse cohort of learners, made me realise why research in this area is so limited and difficult to achieve.
> 3. **Differing views about using a structured approach to the teaching of reading** – Some discussed a difference in understanding what I was doing, others discussed the appropriateness, and some had conflicting views.

This experience has provided me with an understanding of how the teaching of literacy – and specifically reading – is effective for all learners. It is about providing opportunities for learners rather than excluding them. As adults, our views can sometimes limit the experiences and opportunities provided because we do not feel that they may be valid for specific learners.

Ideas in action: case study from a special school

School – Darleen Grimsby, assistant headteacher, Churchill Park Academy.

Context – This special school has 220 pupils from early years through to Year 14.

Intent – Impact of using structured reading framework. As part of our whole school vision and inclusive practice, we changed our curriculum into pathways and looked at how reading could be accessed by every one of our pupils.

Implementation – First, we assess where the readers are in relation to which stage is a 'best fit'. We also look at 'what' they may need and 'how' they access reading.

Stage 1 – Readers may need to access AAC; the symbols are then decided by what they may need. Communication books, boards, and story time are built into their reading. We use the see and learn programme, and also the language experience method. Other pupils may need a bank of words built up through a whole-word approach to build confidence, as well as using initial sounds before moving into phonics.

Stage 2 – Readers access phonics if it is applicable.

Stage 3 – Has a focus on reading comprehension.

Impact – There was a Year 11 student who was unable to access written text. By the end of the year, he had a bank of words, both with symbols and without. He was able to use initial sounds to work out familiar words and was confident in accessing text. There is a Year 10 student who reads through coping mechanisms; after having the confidence to revisit phonics, he was reading Year 1 books. There is a student who was never interested in books; now she reads using language experience method and is interested in making books.

Through targeted approaches, a lot of our older students have been able to access written text in a way that they had not before.

In my training, I emphasise a 'literacy for all' focus, with a wider definition of reading as gaining meaning from some form of stimulus. This means we look at how our learners are reading interactions, people, situations, objects, events, images, and for many, texts. I emphasise an inclusive framework of literacy-rich opportunities and experiences that supports the development of existing practice as part of this, including sensory stories, storytelling, call and response, intensive interaction, choice making/communication approaches, sound discrimination/music-based approaches, multi-sensory activities, and more! As discussed, the use of a more inclusive definition enables us to view reading as a continuum, that learners may begin and end at any point (although do any of us ever end the journey?). This does not imply that we are trying to make cognitive leaps or treat everyone as being able to move along the continuum in a set way, but that all learners are part of this journey.

In my experience in schools, I found that sometimes views that are polarised leave professionals in a position of deciding if a learner should be thought a reader as opposed to considering all learners as readers within their own way. We can then focus on their strengths as a way into the wonderful world of literacy. This may at some point include a more semi-formal approach to reading/phonics if this is appropriate, meaningful, and engaging for the learner.

There are arguments that focus on the relevance of literacy approaches for learners and if time should be spent on more meaningful or functional aspects (Imray, 2021). As with the decision not to include learners in literacy activities, this is something that needs to be reassessed as learners develop, in discussion with parents/carers as to what is the best way forward for that learner at that moment in time.

Finally, I want to emphasise that there is no one answer or scheme that will be the best fit for all learners if we do not include opportunities to experience and develop an understanding about the world of literacy which focuses on the following, then we can never be sure of what might become relevant for that learner.

- Developing shared attention around engaging literacy experiences
- Understanding of narrative
- Development of turn taking
- Awareness of sequence
- Understanding of emotions
- Understanding of the world around us, images, and logograms
- Awareness of pictures, text, and print referencing, along with letters and sounds

The beginning is to promote motivation and engagement in literacy for all learners; the end – that is not yet known!

Research has highlighted that successful inclusive schools start from the curriculum and develop pedagogical approaches to meet the diverse needs of pupils (Lewis & Norwich, 2000; Porter & Lacey, 2005). The continua of teaching approaches proposed by Lewis and Norwich (2000), has been elaborated to include a wider range of SEN groups. Lewis and Norwich (2000) propose that pedagogies vary by intensity of approach along a continuum. Therefore, any adaptation to teaching is not seen as creating a different or specialist approach; rather, it is one aspect of the same underlining pedagogy (Lewis & Norwich, 2000). Today, leaders are faced with decisions regarding the direction of the curriculum for all pupils, specifically those with complex needs. My view is: Why would we limit our curriculum? Why create a narrow view of the world? At this point, academics and professionals may be shouting because pupils need the skills specifically to thrive in the wider community once school is complete. My response would be: Who are we to know what might inspire a child, what may motivate them to attend, respond, communicate, read, write, or interact?

> **Time to think**
>
> Are there any memories that you have that stick out in your mind in terms of learning to read?
>
> Can you think about anything meaningful that helped you to become more engaged in the process or that made you become less engaged?

References

Civinini, C. (2020) *Coping with Covid: Reading key to closing learning gap* [online] Available at: www.tes.com/magazine/archive/coping-covid-reading-key-closing-learning-gap [Accessed: 28/06/2022]

Clark, C. & Picton, I. (2020) *Children and young people's reading in 2020 before and during the COVID-19 lockdown* [online]. National Literacy Trust Research Report Available at: https://cdn.literacytrust.org.uk/media/documents/National_Literacy_Trust_-_Reading_practices_under_lockdown_report_-_FINAL.pdf [Accessed: 27/06/2022]

Cremin, T., Mottram, M., Collins, F., Powell, S. & Safford, K. (2014) *Building Communities of Engaged Readers: Reading for Pleasure*. London: Routledge.

Department for Education (2014) *National curriculum in England: Framework for key stages 1–4* [online] Available at: www.gov.uk/government/collections/national-curriculum [Accessed: 16/05/2022]

Department for Education (2021) *The reading framework: Teaching the foundations of literacy* [online] Available at: www.gov.uk/government/publications/the-reading-framework-teaching-the-foundations-of-literacy [Accessed: 23/06/2022]

Department for Education (2022) *Summary of the SEND review: Right support, right place, right time* [online] Available at: www.gov.uk/government/publications/send-and-ap-green-paper-responding-to-the-consultation/summary-of-the-send-review-right-support-right-place-right-time [Accessed: 12/07/2022]

Government of England (2021) *The engagement model* [online] Available at: www.gov.uk/government/publications/the-engagement-model [Accessed: 19/05/2022]

Imray, P. (2007) *Inclusion: does it matter where pupils are taught?* OFSTED [online] Available at: https://dera.ioe.ac.uk/6001/1/Inclusion%20does%20it%20matter%20where%20pupils%20are%20taught%20%28pdf%20format%29%20.pdf [Accessed: 18/06/2022]

Imray, P. (2021) A different view of literacy. *Support for Learning*, 36, (2) [online] Available at: www.researchgate.net/publication/350756737_A_different_view_of_literacy [Accessed: 27/06/2022]

Kasa-Hendrickson, C. (2005) There's no way this kid's retarded: teachers' optimistic constructions of students' ability. *International Journal of Inclusive Education*, 9, (1), pp. 55–69 Available at: www.tandfonline.com/doi/abs/10.1080/13603110420000253591?journalCode=tied20 [Accessed: 30/06/2022]

Krishnan, S. & Johnson, M.H. (2014) *A review of behavioural and brain development in the early years: The 'toolkit' for later book-related skills* [online] Available at: www.booktrust.org.uk/globalassets/resources/research/krishnan-johnson-2014-full-report-a-review-of-behavioural-and-brain-development-in-the-early-years-the-toolkit-for-later-book-related-skills-.pdf [Accessed: 19/07/2022]

Lacey, P. (2001) The role of learning support assistants in the inclusive learning of pupils with severe and profound learning difficulties. *Educational Review*, 53, (2), pp. 157–167 Available at: www.tandfonline.com/doi/abs/10.1080/00131910120055589 [Accessed: 28/06/2022]

Lewis, A. & Norwich, B. (2000) *Mapping a Pedagogy for Special Educational Needs*. Exeter: University of Exeter.

Longhorn, F. (2001) *Literacy for Very Special People*. Catalyst Education Resources Ltd. Available at https://sites.google.com/view/flolonghornsensorybooksfreedow/home#h.j3m1v4enpi7s

Male, D.B. & Rayner, M.R. (2007). Who goes to SLD schools? Aspects of policy and provision for pupils with profound and multiple learning difficulties who attend special schools in England. *Support for Learning*, 22, 3, pp. 145–152 [online] Available at: https://nasenjournals.onlinelibrary.wiley.com/doi/abs/10.1111/j.1467-9604.2007.00462.x [Accessed: 30/06/2022]

Moseley, S. (2009) *The effect of reading instruction on the self-concept and self-esteem of pupils with severe learning disabilities*. Ph.D. Thesis. University of London Institute of Education.

OECD. (2002) *Reading for change: Performance and engagement across countries* [online] Available at: www.oecd.org/education/school/programmeforinternationalstudentassessmentpisa/33690904.pdf [Accessed: 23/07/2022]

Ofsted (2019) *Education inspection framework* [online]. Department for Education. Available at: www.gov.uk/government/publications/education-inspection-framework [Accessed: 09/06/2022]

Porter, J. & Lacey, P. (2005) *Researching Learning Difficulties: A Guide for Practitioners*. Sage.

Science Daily. (2019) *A 'million word gap' for children who aren't read to at home* [online]. Ohio State University. Available at: www.sciencedaily.com/releases/2019/04/190404074947.htm [Accessed: 19/06/2022]

2 Where to begin and the importance of high expectations

In this chapter, we will consider what is required to create an inclusive reading curriculum framework. The emphasis will be on the building blocks that are necessary to ensure that all learners, including those with complex needs, have rich literacy opportunities and experiences to support the development of reading skills. It is often the case that when pupils struggle with specific aspects, there is a tendency to give them more of the same, supporting deficits through repetition. This may mean that the curriculum offered can become further narrowed and there is less opportunity to develop other skills, motivation, and meaningful engagement. One of the findings of my research was that often learners with complex needs receive limited literacy curriculum due to many factors including time, beliefs, and an understanding about how children learn to read. Raising expectations and providing access to literacy at any age can make a difference to the lives of all learners. So how do we do this? The significance of everyone viewing reading as a priority across the school and wider community is highlighted as key to success for all.

My beliefs at the start of my career had been relatively focused and I entered the special school context after several years teaching in mainstream primary schools. Prior to this, I had some experience of special schools through voluntary positions and my role as a teaching assistant within a special school after I had completed my psychology degree. I began working as a literacy coordinator and class teacher within key stage three in a large special school in London. Within six months of this role, my view around the teaching of literacy became clouded. I was met with some mixed feedback internally about the relevance of some of the approaches to the teaching of reading that I was using. This was in contradiction to external inspections, achievements of my class, and feedback from families which had been extremely positive. I was left wondering where to go next and how to ensure that I was providing the best opportunities for the learners I was working with.

I embarked on my master's degree which then led me onto my PhD. Both consolidated my thinking about the teaching of reading, yet when I finished them, it was like I was back at the beginning. The writing of this book has been an interesting process full of stops and starts. I had an interesting exchange on Twitter one evening which led me to begin or at least find a place to start once more. The useful piece of advice was you do not need to have all the answers, just take a step forward and then another one; it is the lifting of the foot to take the step that makes the difference. So, this is the next bit.

An inclusive view of reading

In terms of the teaching of reading to learners with complex needs, there are several views focused on the appropriateness, relevance, and content of the curriculum offered. One of the most frequently discussed arguments is: Should we should be debating ways into reading for learners with complex needs at all? There is a view held that the teaching of reading is not something which is achievable by a small group of learners with the most profound complex needs. The definition of who this small group is and where the edges of the group may be can lead to confusion. This view may become applied to a larger group of learners and confuse this issue, making it difficult for those new to the profession to move forward with ideas around an area that is deemed to be inappropriate.

My view is that we should promote this as a more inclusive construct, as opposed to an area where there is some form of catching up. Literacy is at the heart of education; everything that we do revolves around the development of the ability to understand and communicate about the world around us. With the rise in technology, communication, and different ways to understand the world, literacy can be conceptualised in a much broader way. This leads to the question: How can removing literacy from the general conversation about the curriculum that we offer to all learners be supportive or inclusive?

DOI: 10.4324/9781003220046-3

22 *Where to begin and the importance of high expectations*

> **Ideas in action: case study from a special school**
>
> **School** – Jeff Daniel Highshore School, Camberwell, London.
>
> **Context** – This year we began providing our Year 7 pupils with specific literacy sessions as part of their weekly timetable.
>
> **Intent** – To increase access to literacy-rich opportunities and support confidence in all learners.
>
> **Implementation** – This shift in the curriculum offers includes a daily focus on reading and sharing books across all genres (real and technology-based), structured phonics sessions, and more!
>
> **Impact** – The pupils have embraced it with enthusiasm and the impact this has had is amazing. I am secondary trained and have learnt so much about the process of learning to read this year, I can see the possible impact that it has had on learners. Our primary colleagues have taken to the introduction of a structured phonics approach like a duck to water, and the pupils are flying!

Over the past three years, I have faced a considerable amount of change, the biggest of which was starting my own company as an independent consultant working with professionals and families across education. My specific focus is on raising outcomes for learners with complex needs. During this period, I have been able to read more, talk more, and network with some incredibly enthusiastic professionals. I have been reminded of why I am so passionate about this area and why I had spent years working hard to make a difference. Several years ago, I read an article in the *Guardian* about a young man named Jonathan Bryan.

Jonathan's story

Jonathan had written a book called *Eye Can Write* (Bryan, 2018). This was not surprising until you saw a photo of Jonathan (Figure 2.1) and read that he spent a large part of his life in a special needs school, in a class where he was referred to as having profound and multiple learning difficulties.

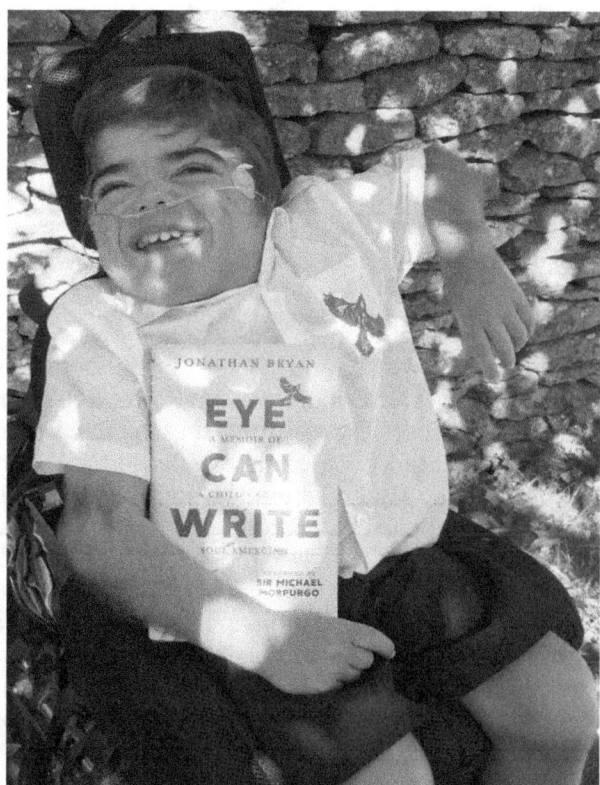

Figure 2.1 Jonathan Bryan.

This book and a later meeting with Jonathan gave me the inspiration and drive to write this book. His story had reignited a flame that I felt had been extinguished after many years working as a headteacher of a fast-paced school. I realised that my vision and reason for entering the profession had been worn away. The challenges I faced daily had left little time for inspirational or strategic leadership. I had started to fail at making a difference and influencing the views of others positively. I had spent many years previously researching and demonstrating the importance of teaching reading to all pupils, yet within my own school, the teaching of reading was only just gaining momentum.

> **Jonathan's story**
>
> The story told by Jonathan was one of overcoming barriers to communicate what he was able to do and demonstrating to others the way in which he could access learning. Jonathan had been labelled prior to starting school, and although these labels are sometimes needed, they can then become barriers. I recommend that this book is shared with all staff and extracts used in training or meetings to ensure we all remember the importance of seeing every child as an individual, rather than the label that has been applied to them. The important message provided to us by Jonathan's story is that it is up to us to consider what the barriers to learning might be and look at ways to reduce these. I have since had the opportunity to work closely with the charity Teach Us Too, Jonathan and his mum Chantal. Teach Us Too is focused on "promoting an education system where all children are taught literacy regardless of their label" (https://www.teachustoo.org.uk/).

Jonathan, like many pupils, specifically those with additional needs, had worked hard to overcome many barriers to learning; his journey was supported and made possible by the belief of the adults around him. The story of Jonathan is one that may be rare and may not reflect a large percentage of those learners whose needs have been categorised as profound and multiple learning difficulties. This is not the important part of the story. What it highlights is that when we make assumptions about the needs of our learners, this can lead to a reduction of the opportunities and experiences that are provided to them. This then leads to a change in our expectations of what may be important or relevant. There are learners with a huge variety of complex needs in schools across the UK for whom the barriers to learning have not been found, and it is only through a change in our perception of what might be relevant and engaging for those learners that they will then be provided with opportunities to demonstrate this. For some, finding the barrier to learning may lead to progress beyond expectations!

An important question that was posed to Jonathan and his team, during one of the training events – attended by parents, carers, teachers, occupational therapists, and educational psychologists – was: How can the cultures of schools be changed to make sure there is time to ensure everyone has access to learning? The answer from Jonathan was clear: Just start from the belief that everyone can learn and go from there. What else are schools for? Novel idea! Find out more about Teach Us Too at www.teachustoo.org.uk/.

> **Ideas in action: case study from a special school**
>
> **School** – Mrs Connacher, principal and teacher.
>
> **Context** – Croftcroighn Primary School is purpose-built to meet the needs of children with complex additional support needs, including cognitive, sensory, communication and physical impairments from P1–P7. The school also has a nursery which admits children from the age of 2 years. There are currently 61 pupils attending the school. This pupil is 6 years old and his main modes of communication are body language, vocalisation and a few words such as "no".
>
> **Intent** – Using a pupil's interest as a vehicle for literacy development to improve engagement and the transfer of skills across contexts.
>
> **Implementation** – We were encouraging him to identify his own picture during class routines and this was proving difficult, even though we knew he was very aware of his peers

> and liked to watch them throughout the day. He was also interested in flicking through apps on the iPad, so I used Choice Board Creator to create a choice board where he was asked to "find Harry" and was then rewarded with an applause from the app.
>
> **Impact** – Through a change in all approach expectations, we discovered that not only did he know the names of all the pupils in the class, but he knew the names of staff members, as well! Photographs were continued to be used in conjunction with the technology around the class. As part of our Mother's Day celebrations, I sent a collage to all the parents via our digital diaries and his mum was absolutely delighted. She wrote back to tell us that he had verbally named all the pupils from their photographs and he had said his own name for the first time, bringing her to tears! I wanted to make the most of his developing literacy and communication skills.

Building blocks needed to create an inclusive reading framework

So where do we begin when we think about teaching reading? During my training, I use an infographic that depicts a series of building blocks. These are the key elements that should be considered when looking at how to begin and continue with the journey of teaching learners with complex needs to read. Figure 2.2 illustrates the key aspects that are established as essential to this journey. This is based on key research focusing on reading development, developed using evidence from the body of knowledge referred to as the science of reading, most recently summarised in the reading framework (DfE, 2021), my experience within special education, my own research, and the experiences and impact evidenced by professionals currently working within special schools across the UK.

Building blocks needed for an inclusive reading framework

These building blocks are not in a specific chronological order, but are the foundations that need to be in place to ensure that all learners are provided with the opportunities to become a reader.

- **High expectations** – This aspect refers to us and how we define reading and include it within the curriculum, as something that all learners can embark on.
- **Rich literacy environment** – Refers to all of the experiences and opportunities that we provide for learners to support their awareness and understanding of the link between language and text. If we think about typically developing young children, they are immersed in an environment often prior to birth whereby they are exposed to many opportunities to understand this relationship between language and print.
- **Understanding of how reading develops** – This is important, as it is through this understanding that we are able to use existing knowledge and good practise to support all learners. It supports a move away from a resource- or strategy-driven curriculum to understanding

Figure 2.2 The building blocks needed for all learners.

why certain activities and resources are useful, and how they support the process of learning to read.
- **Word recognition and language comprehension** – Refers to the importance of all learners having the opportunity to develop both of these aspects within an inclusive reading framework. This will be explored further in the book.
- **Assessment** – In any area of the curriculum, assessment has a key role. It is supporting us to be aware of the learner's strengths and motivations, as well as gaps in their understanding or development. We will discuss how to use strengths as a starting point to build on and develop learners' skills.
- **Regular structured literacy opportunities** – Refers to the opportunities and experiences provided to learners with complex needs as part of an inclusive reading framework. I will use the model proposed by Koppenhaver and Erickson in their *Comprehensive Literacy for All* book to illustrate the importance of providing access to all elements of literacy including shared reading, alphabet activities, writing and independent reading.
- **Accessibility** – This is the golden thread that runs through all of the blocks. The importance of accessibility (learners being able to participate and access all activities) is fundamental to everything that we do.

High expectations

The term "inclusive literacy" was used by Penny Lacey to refer to practices that were not about the teaching of reading or writing (Lacey et al., 2007). This is an interesting contradiction of terms referring to something that is inclusive as not being about reading, but where do we begin and where do we stop when we talk about the teaching of reading? Certainly, when we consider a young baby, the experiences we provide would be classed as inclusive literacy experiences, but we do consider them as separate to the teaching that then leads to the teaching of reading. Literacy is learnt through interaction with and exposure to all aspects of literacy.

The start of any journey is the need for high expectations, or at least the need to see reading as something that all learners can embark on. If we view school as something which is preparing us for the future in terms of academic achievement, we may be forced into a narrow definition of what being literate and what the teaching of literacy means for learners with complex needs. If we view literacy and being literate as something which relates to increasing opportunities for learners to engage with the world, to communicate, and to have a greater understanding of themselves and the world around them, we can define and think about literacy in a wider, more inclusive way.

High expectations for all refers to a belief that everyone can achieve in their own way. The expectation is not that learners will be forced to make a cognitive leap or achieve in a more formal way. The inclusion of all learners into an inclusive reading framework is not an ableist or competency-based approach; it is a way of making the whole literacy curriculum accessible to all. It is the linking of aspects of the curriculum, rather than seeing them as separate and therefore not to be discussed in relation to each other. The notion of high expectations for all learners is that we will provide a literacy-rich environment whereby they are part of the whole curriculum with specific personalised aspects for key learning to take place. The notion of an inclusive framework opens, rather than closes, what we are offering to all learners. It is not an expectation that all learners will learn to read and write in a conventional way if we just keep going; the presumption is that the reading curriculum can be one that learners access within their own pathways, that each of these pathways is linked to an overarching framework that provides possibilities and enriches the lives of all learners.

The use of the term high expectations refers to us changing the way that we think and look at our reading curriculum to consider what the experiences should be for learners within the earliest stages of development. If we consider the early reading experiences that we provide to very young typically developing learners, we can see that these are provided with very little expectation or assessment of understanding. We read, sing, and share books to create enjoyable experiences that everyone will find engaging or interesting. This can happen from a very early age. Research demonstrates that in many cases babies less than 6 months old are surrounded by experiences of being read to, sung to, and shown picture books with very little expectation that they will suddenly read any of the words. There are many examples that have been shared with me throughout my research for this book when professionals have just started to engage in play-based exploration using learner's interests, increasing access to text in meaningful contexts.

> ### Ideas in action: case study from a special school
>
> **Context** – Adele Hughes shared within the Facebook group.
> **Intent** – I have started looking at the wider picture and opportunities for literacy in everyday exploration and play.
> **Implementation** – One child has taken a liking to Paddington Bear jigsaws. We made up the four sizes and started naming things in the jigsaw.
> **Impact** – As the pupil is non-verbal, they started taking my hand to verbally label objects and characters. I then introduced "Where is . . . ?" The pupil is now taking my hand to point to it. I am hoping to build on this in coming weeks and use it as my little case study! Thanks so much for widening my mind through this training.

Our role

If we think about the practice of sharing books with very young babies, we know that this is part of the process of providing a rich literacy environment whereby everyone is an emergent reader. The reason these experiences are appropriate is that they have a key role to play in the development of early reading skills. These experiences are invaluable to support neurological development and connections within our brain. They support our understanding about the link between language and print; even if this is where our learners remain, they will have an increased understanding about the world around them. The question is: Why would this be different in terms of learners who require the most intense learning experiences, who are within the early stages of cognitive development? The decision has been made at some point, but these experiences may not be appropriate or useful to the learner once they enter education and their curriculum becomes narrowed.

As with every aspect of the curriculum, we would consider how to ensure that the experiences provided are age and stage appropriate. For young children, simple story books may be appropriate, but for older learners who are at these early stages of literacy development, non-fiction books related to areas of interest or about the learner themselves would be more appropriate. There are many engaging picture books available for older learners; I recommend e books available for older learners and I recommend looking at the list provided by Simon Smith on his blog www.smithsmm.wordpress.com/2016/12/11/picture-this-why-i-love-picture-books/.

All learners, including those with complex needs, must have the opportunity to be immersed in language-rich experiences whereby participation, engagement, and enjoyment of literacy occurs on a regular basis. The importance here is focused on the culture of the classroom and school, the importance of high aspirations/expectations, literacy-rich environments, and the impact that a simple change in our attitude can have on the outcomes for learners with complex needs.

To become literate, there needs to be an understanding of how literacy can develop differently for all learners – including those with complex needs. There needs to be a clear understanding of how to support making the literacy world as accessible as possible. Central to the 'intent' aspect of the EIF is that staff are determined that all learners can succeed. If we want learners to become readers and access a wide range of literature, we must believe they can and provide opportunities for this.

The key here is us; we are the ones to make a difference. For learners with more complex learning needs, the emphasis on us is even greater. This requires flexibility and adaptation of traditional approaches to support the removal of barriers to learning that may exist. For example, young children develop an interest in stories through repeated exposure to their favourite books. For learners with more complex needs, we need to facilitate opportunities for this.

It is the role of us as professionals to be the person that carries out actions to make a difference to our pupils, no matter how small. A story that has become the ethos behind my current professional role is that of the star thrower. It has been adapted by many from "The Star Thrower" by Loren C. Eiseley (1978) and is often used by motivational speakers. This story is about a child walking along the beach after a storm and throwing back starfish that had been left as the tide had gone out. The child is asked why they are taking the time to throw back a small number of the many starfish left, as what difference can it make? The child responds that it made a difference to that starfish. The point of the story was that every action, no matter how small can make a difference to learners. It is a story I have told in assemblies and has remained with me after many years; it is also the reason for the starfish in my logo.

Figure 2.3 Picture of a starfish.

Figure 2.4 My logo containing a starfish.

The message "it made a difference to that one" is one we need to embed in all schools. It is our role to change the culture of schools through changing the perspectives of the adults within it. As leaders, we have a role in creating organisations where we believe in our pupils, instilling a growth mindset culture whereby pupils in turn believe in themselves. The Pygmalion effect is a well-researched phenomenon whereby teacher's expectations had been found to correlate highly with pupil performance. It is the leaders who create the context that influence teacher/staff expectations, so let's all be the leader who believes, the leader who makes the least restrictive assumption that everyone can learn anything.

When pupils struggle with specific aspects, there is a tendency to give them more of the same, supporting the deficits through repetition. The problem comes when you look at what is being offered to pupils: Are we narrowing the curriculum in such a way as to reduce rather than enhance opportunities for pupils to gain knowledge skills and understanding? Research by Stanovich (1986) used the term "Matthew effect" when discussing reading opportunities and environments provided for children with complex needs. This is referred to within the reading framework (gov.uk, 2021). The term is a reference to the Gospel according to Matthew. The story tells of the rich getting richer and the poor being left to become even poorer. He applied this idea to the educational opportunities offered to struggling readers (Stanovich, 1986).

Children become confident readers through reading. Unfortunately, poor readers may never achieve this confidence (Clay, 2000; Stanovich, 1993/4). The initial underlying cause of their reading problem can result in reading becoming a slow, laborious, and unrewarding task, which leads to a lack of motivation or even fear of future reading activities (Stanovich, 1993/4). This can become a downward spiral, whereby future experiences with reading reinforce existing negative feelings. The result is that the less the children learn, the less they are able to learn due to an impoverished knowledge base and opportunities.

> **My experience and the importance of relationships**
>
> During my career and research, I have struggled with reading, writing, and – in the past – public speaking. My difficulties were supported and overcome by the beliefs shown and relationships I had with people around me. I have always had problems with spelling, and I am unable to visualise how a word is spelt or see incorrectly spelt words within my own writing. One mistake I made motivated my research thesis and further interest in the teaching of reading and writing, as well as strengthened my faith in people. It related to my use of the word 'potential' within a nerve-racking presentation. During my NPQH course, I used this word in my 'vision for leadership' presentation. It appeared ten times – and unbeknown to me, I had misspelt it on every slide. My wonderful group ignored this, clapping in support and filling me with praise once I had finished. Only at the very end of the session did one of my friends take me to one side and tell me in future this is how you spell 'potential'! The support and beliefs of others keep us alive and passionate. We never stop learning and I have spent many years using my own learning needs to become a better teacher. Today, I would probably be classed as having dyslexia. I spent many years avoiding writing in front of others or on a whiteboard. This is quite a task for a primary school teacher and later a trainer of large groups of educationalists! Luckily word processors and all forms of assistive technology have meant that completing my PhD and continuing to publish was not as hard as it could have been.

> **Ideas in action: case study from a special school**
>
> **School** – Naomi Austin, literacy lead at Beaucroft Foundation School.
>
> **Context** – Beaucroft Foundation School is a special school in Dorset that caters to children and young people between the ages of 4 and 19 who are experiencing learning difficulties, including complex needs, and those with an Autistic Spectrum Disorder. There are currently 165 pupils on roll, and the school will be expanding to include a new college site in the coming year, bringing our numbers up to a maximum of 245 running from 4–19 years.
>
> **Intent** – We enhanced our literacy curriculum, and in doing so, gave teachers the confidence to try reading and writing activities with learners they would not have previously.
>
> **Implementation and Impact** – This may have been seen as controversial with some initially, but as staff began to embrace the approach, it has been a real eye opener! Learners have been using post boxes, sensory trays, water guns, fly swatters, switches, jumping mats, sound boards, recordable postcards, and self-authored books to engage and involve all, and it has been both wonderful and surprising in terms of the impact on learners' engagement and understanding!

Final thoughts

As educators, we provided pupils with the means to access learning. Do we know what they might need to support this? Do pupils have the confidence to try, or the ability to process the information in the way it is being presented? Do we need to consider what adaptations we may need to make, which could be as simple as providing time to process the information we are presenting? Research has found that, on average, pupils take 7 seconds to process verbal information in a classroom; consider how long you provide people with before you move on. We will discuss the importance of access later in this book, but for now, remember it is us who hold the key to considering ways forward for each learner.

> **Time to reflect**
>
> Think of a time your views influenced your actions. Consider your current perspective and those around you: How does that influence the curriculum that you provide?

References

Byran, J. (2018) *Eye Can Write: A Memoir of a Child's Silent Soul Emerging*. London: Lagom.

Clay, M. (2000) *The Concepts about Print Test*. Portsmouth, NH: Heinemann.

Department for Education. (2021) *The reading framework: Teaching the foundations of literacy* [online] Available at: www.gov.uk/government/publications/the-reading-framework-teaching-the-foundations-of-literacy [Accessed: 23/06/2022]

Eiseley, L.C. (1978) *The Star Thrower*. New York, London, Toronto, Sydney: Harper Perennial.

gov.uk (2021) The reading framework: Teaching the foundations of literacy. Available at: https://www.gov.uk/government/publications/the-reading-framework-teaching-the-foundations-of-literacy

Lacey, P., Layton, L., Miller, C., Goldbart, J. & Lawson, H. (2007) What is literacy for students with severe learning difficulties? Exploring conventional and inclusive literacy. *Journal of Research in Special Educational Needs*, 7, (3), pp. 149–160 [online] Available at: https://citeseerx.ist.psu.edu/viewdoc/download?doi=10.1.1.672.2404&rep=rep1&type=pdf [Accessed: 16/07/2022]

Stanovich, K. (1986) Matthew effects in reading: Some consequences of individual differences in the acquisition of literacy. *Reading Research Quarterly*, 21, (4), pp. 360–407 [online] Available at: www.researchgate.net/publication/230853161_Matthew_Effects_in_Reading_Some_Consequences_of_Individual_Differences_in_the_Acquisition_of_Literacy [Accessed: 15/07/2022]

Stanovich, K. (1993) Romance and reality. *The Reading Teacher*, 47, (4), pp. 280–291 [online] Available at: www.keithstanovich.com/Site/Research_on_Reading_files/RdTch93.pdf [Accessed: 09/06/2022]

3 The importance of accessible literacy-rich environments

The building blocks discussed in the previous chapter contain a brick that highlights the crucial role of a literacy-rich environment. In this chapter, we discuss why rich literacy environments are fundamental to all learners, including those with complex needs. We will discuss the importance of providing all learners with opportunities to be immersed in accessible, rich literacy experiences whereby they gain an understanding about language and its link to print/text. We will explore how to bridge our sensory curriculum and access to an understanding of print to support all learners. We will discuss the importance of enriching the sensory curriculum to develop an understanding about print in a meaningful and contextualised way. Finally, we discuss the importance of widening our definition of what reading means for our most complex learners, to ensure that our curriculum framework is inclusive of all.

As we have discussed in previous chapters, if we begin to exclude aspects from learners' experiences and environments, we need to decide that this will not be relevant to the learners accessing those experiences or environments. Would it not be more inclusive to create links between the well-developed sensory curriculum and an inclusive reading framework, providing all learners with the opportunity to be readers in the widest sense? This would be achieved by providing opportunities to experience and understand language and its meaning in many ways.

1. Develop an awareness, tolerance and understanding of language and sound
2. Develop an understanding of the relationship between language, objects, pictures, and print
3. Develop an understanding of the relationship between language and text/print

The curriculum offered to learners at a more pre-formal and early semi-formal level is one that is founded on sensory experiences and opportunities. This may take the form of sensory stories, immersive experiences, intensive interaction, senseology-based opportunities, and more. What is often missing is the inclusion of print and the relationship between letters and sounds, referred to as the alphabetic code. This may be seen as something that is not relevant or appropriate for these learners, but its exclusion means that it may never be relevant for the learner. The discussion is not based on flooding the environment or experiencing it with text but using the additional information it provides as another route for information to reach long-term memory. I will discuss this in more detail further on in the book when I look at the 'Reading Rope' and the wheel of foundation skills that I propose link with the strands of word recognition and language comprehension.

> **Print referencing**
>
> Print referencing has a key role to play in the curriculum for learners in the early years of mainstream education. It is the understanding that print contains meaning, and it is the development of the understanding of the symbolic representation that exists. Print referencing plays an important role, as it enables learners to build awareness of print awareness skills. Learners are drawn into the print around them, enabling them to provide meaning and to make connections between oral and written information. This is a bridge to early reading and writing of text, but it is fundamentally the development of understanding about the world around us. Research using visual scanning technology to track where learners looked most of the time found that prior to print references, learners were visually attending to the page and faces seen. The research found that print referencing had become established within teaching (e.g., pointing out that Max begins with an 'm'); it was found that the learners looked at the face and then at the print that was pointed to (Erickson & Koppenhaver, 2020). As summed up by Heath (1983) states that typically developing learners have over 1,000 hours of time they have encountered print in meaningful contexts.

Print, as we discussed previously in this book, surrounds all of us. If we ignore the existence of print and the role that it plays within the environment and lives of all learners, we are ignoring a key part of the learner's world. There are many specific words which may be meaningful to learners – for example, their name – but we do not provide any opportunities for this learning to be realised. The decision to take this more inclusive model of the teaching of reading will be influenced by the role of high expectations of the adults around the learner.

> **Ideas in action: case study from a special school**
>
> **School** – Jessica Webb, assistant headteacher, Bedelsford School, Surrey.
>
> **Context** – Our school is for students aged 2½–19 who have a wide range of physical disabilities including those with profound and multiple learning difficulties, moderate learning difficulties and complex health needs. However, we are a changing population and many of our pupils now have complex learning difficulties and disabilities (CLDD).
>
> **Intent** – Developing our literacy and specifically reading curriculum with an emphasis on starting from where learners are, and having the confidence to know this.
>
> **Implementation** – This has meant that we have used the training and ideas suggested to enhance our reading curriculum. We have developed our reading policy to highlight the importance of every child being seen as a reader and shared ideas with class teams on how we can implement this. We have adopted the reading stages for readers and now use this language.
>
> Within my own teaching practice and whilst supporting colleagues, I have been able to develop how we can adapt our phonics scheme to suit AAC users to express their learning. Within this, teams have become more confident in leading shared reading sessions and through supporting early writing through the use of predictable word charts.
>
> **Impact** – As a result of these changes, students have been able to access new and revised sessions. Since developing our resonance board sessions, students learning on our pre-formal pathway have been able to experience sessions to support their auditory discrimination, memory, and sequencing skills. Students have been motivated and highly engaged in the sessions leading to deeper learning.

The aspect of print referencing has been something which many schools and classes have begun to look at differently. During one of my training sessions in one special school classroom where learners were predominantly referred to as having profound multiple learning difficulties, the teacher commented that they had begun to use learners' names printed alongside the pictures during circle and personal care time. They were aware that one of the learners was able to recognise the bowl that was used during teeth brushing, even though it was the same colour as the bowl that was used for another member of the class. The teacher wanted to find out if the learner was able to recognise his name that was written on it. In other classes, they have found that there is a definite recognition of learners' printed names when they have begun to use these throughout the day. The important aspect of this is that by incorporating key print in a meaningful context, the opportunity was presented for a deeper understanding about the link between language and print; there was no expectation or assessing, just an enrichment of the environment to include meaningful core text.

The importance of language

A rich literacy environment provides learners with opportunities to experience and be immersed in language that is different from that which is used during our communication exchanges. The language that learners are exposed to – during stories, poetry, or other forms of interesting and informative text – is far richer. As described by James Britton (1972), reading and writing can be seen to float on a sea of talk. Much of the curriculum for learners within pre-formal or early developmental curriculum frameworks consist of activities and approaches based on engagement with the world around them developing communication. To communicate, we must be aware of others and want to interact.

> **Ideas in action: case study from a special school**
>
> **School** – Mrs Connacher, principal teacher, Croftcroighn School. An all-age special school for learners with complex additional support needs, including cognitive, sensory, communication and physical impairments from P1–P7. The school also has a nursery which admits children from the age of 2 years. There are currently 61 pupils attending the school.
>
> **Context** – I am a teacher in a school for pupils with complex learning needs. There are currently seven pupils in the class, and their ages range from 3–7 years old. Five of the pupils have a diagnosis of autism spectrum disorder (ASD) and two have more complex physical needs including cerebral palsy and cortical visual impairment. There are currently four staff working with the pupils; two teachers who job-share, a child development officer and two support for learning workers.
>
> **Intent** – To increase access to stories for all learners, using a group sensory story session, which included motivating props and text.
>
> **Implementation** – The class theme for the term was the city of Glasgow, and I was keen to use a sensory story that reflected the experiences that you would have if you were to do a city tour. I found an online sensory story of a dog that was lost in London and adapted this to suit the new location. Local landmarks were listed and the class team put together ideas of sensory experiences that would include sights, smells, textures, and sounds of the city. The staff had used pupil motivators when they selected the props and the flowers were included to help involve one of our more difficult to engage pupils as he really likes to hold and smell plants. The frequency of story sessions was also increased from once a week to at least twice to allow the pupils more opportunities to become familiar with the story, to build anticipation, and to develop consistent responses to the props and text.
>
> **Impact** – We found that the class was calmer and provided a better setting for those who require longer time for processing and responding to the story. We were able to observe responses for the pupils, and they began to develop some anticipation during the story, which was so lovely to witness. This change in approach led to increased engagement from all pupils.

Sharing stories

The reading framework (DfE, 2021) discusses the crucial role that is played by stories and talking about stories. The link between stories and the development of the learner's vocabulary and language is highlighted. Each page of a story contains a new place to explore in our minds, to engage and motivate all learners. Mary Myatt has written some incredibly powerful literature around the importance of the curriculum and ensuring breath for all. As Mary Myatt states, "Stories help pupils to make sense of new content, they help pupils to make connections and finally they are enjoyable!" (Myatt, 2020).

Activities that are based on a shared knowledge are central to this.

Reading provides the perfect vehicle for all learning through
- Sharing of stories, poems songs, narrative, storytelling, sensory stories, and more
- Creating choice-making opportunities based on experiences they have enjoyed
- Providing a focus on turn taking in a realistic context
- Using books (in the widest sense, to include technology and sensory stories) to create shared attention activities
- Providing rich experiences for repetitive activities that build up a desire for more

These experiences support an awareness of meaning, where connections between text/story/object/interaction and own experience/understanding are made. The basis of these experiences is the sending and receiving of signals through a shared interest. Literacy activities can provide concrete language-embedded experiences including listening, comprehension, vocabulary, and use of narrative, all of which are key to the development of communication for learners with complex needs. At all times, learners need to be provided with accessible and appropriate environments whereby strategies may need to be even more focused to ensure that they can develop and gain the skills.

> **A community of story sharers**
>
> I recently met with Pie Corbett and Jonathan Bryan to discuss ways forward in terms of promoting literacy for all. During the conversation, we discussed the importance of stories and how they create a way to bind us together, and how they can be something that we instantly have in common. Pie reflected on the notion that almost all communication is a story; our conversations, interactions, and events all relate to some form of story. This conversation continued to strengthen the foundation of this book – that all learners must have the opportunity to be part of this community of storytellers and story sharers.

Making your own books

The power of storytelling and narrative is culturally and historically proven as a powerful way for us all to learn (Grove, 2022). Through becoming storytellers, we strengthen connections in our brain, leading to physical changes. A powerful way to support the development of literacy for all learners is to support them to develop an awareness of stories both within and around them. We need to ensure that our libraries, reading material, and texts contain personalised representations based on experiences of all learners. By creating personalised representations based on experiences, we have access to stories and text which engage and motivate. These can be written or recorded in many ways using apps (Book Creator, Clicker, Pictello), photos, recording devices, story boxes, boards, talkers, grids, and more based on the learner's interests and experiences.

> **Ideas in action: case study from a special school**
>
> **School** – Ceri Cusack, SEND Teacher special school.
>
> **Context** – My team and I identified that pupils enjoyed looking at photos of themselves whilst actively learning.
>
> **Intent** – Using photos to promote engagement and participation in literacy activities including sharing books, creating a two-way reading dialogue.
>
> **Implementation** – This started as photos on displays and sharing photos taken on the iPad for observational evidence. Supporting adults would narrate what the pupils had been doing, using names, adjectives, tone of voice, and backing up the narration with the pupil's preferred method of communication (verbal, Makaton, gestures, cues, supporting symbols to match if appropriate). As all the resources to support were already present in my class, this was an easy 'grab and go' type of activity that could occur ad hoc during self-initiated play/learning.
>
> As we went into the next academic year, I collected photos of pupils' active learning and engagement, popped them into an MS Word document, printed them and laminated them. Each pupil had their own photo on the front, the same image used for their daily routine timetable. This gave opportunities for pupils to choose the friend they wanted to 'read' about or find their own book. Each term, a new book was created and the results remained the same – high engagement, calm, conversation with support staff, increase in use of Makaton signs, and a sheer enjoyment of looking back on the work they had completed.

> **Impact** – We found that even the students who are hardest to engage due to behaviour and concentration challenges would sit and 'chat' about the photos for long periods of time, pointing at the photos and looking at the supporting adult to show understanding of a two-way 'reading' dialogue. For pupils emerging onto the communication continuum, where photos and objects of reference were their go-to method of communication, the books helped develop the idea of turning pages, selecting features to discuss by eye pointing or finger pointing and the idea of 'to and fro' conversation for reading. This supported developing the use of symbol communication books. On a wellbeing front, time to be calm could be a rare occurrence for some of my cohort – time to make positive relationships with new staff and to feel safe, secure, and nurtured whilst immersing themselves in the pages of a familiar, already experienced, real-life context book.

The process of creating your own book is something that can be accessible, relevant, and engaging for learners of all ages. Learners' own books can be used to support all aspects of literacy from understanding the sequence, purpose, and way that books work to the development of an understanding of letter sound correspondence, language structure, and the link between speech, written language, and comprehension. Infographic Figure 3.1 from CALL Scotland illustrates the process of creating your own book either physically or digitally to support all learners.

Sensory stories

The important golden thread that links access to a literacy-rich environment for learners with the most complex needs is the use of sensory-focused approaches to increase engagement and participation. Sensory stories are an ingrained part of every classroom for learners with complex needs. The issue is: Why and how do we make the most of these powerful resources? In many special schools, learners who are working within the pre-formal curriculum will have sensory stories on their timetable on a regular basis.

> **Ideas in action: case study from a special school**
>
> **School** – Delamere School, @DelamereSchool.
>
> **Context** – Delamere School is a community-maintained specialist primary school. We have 110 places with additional nursery provision for children with complex learning needs including learning difficulty, autism, Down's syndrome, sensory impairments and developmental delay.
>
> **Intent** – During our reading for pleasure sessions, we are looking at the African story "Kofi and the Magic Shaker" using sensory resources exploring the warmth of the African sun, the coconut trees, and the shaker which is a gift from a spider.
>
> **Implementation** – As part of their sensory room session the children in Caterpillar Class have been exploring 'Underwater animals' book. The children have to use a torch to find different animals hidden inside the book.
>
> **Impact** – We have had some great engagement from the children, and they have used language to identify what they have found.

The power of sensory stories is now being realised as appropriate for learners of all abilities and ages; they enable stories to be brought to life and provide opportunities for information to be encoded and accessible to learners in many multi-sensory ways.

- A sensory story enables a framework for repetition, alongside the introduction of new vocabulary and ideas.
- They enable all people to access a story, to experience some form of cause and effect, or to pick up on parts of an activity and begin to predict what might happen next.
- Sensory stories enable repetition of familiar language within a routine or familiar structure.

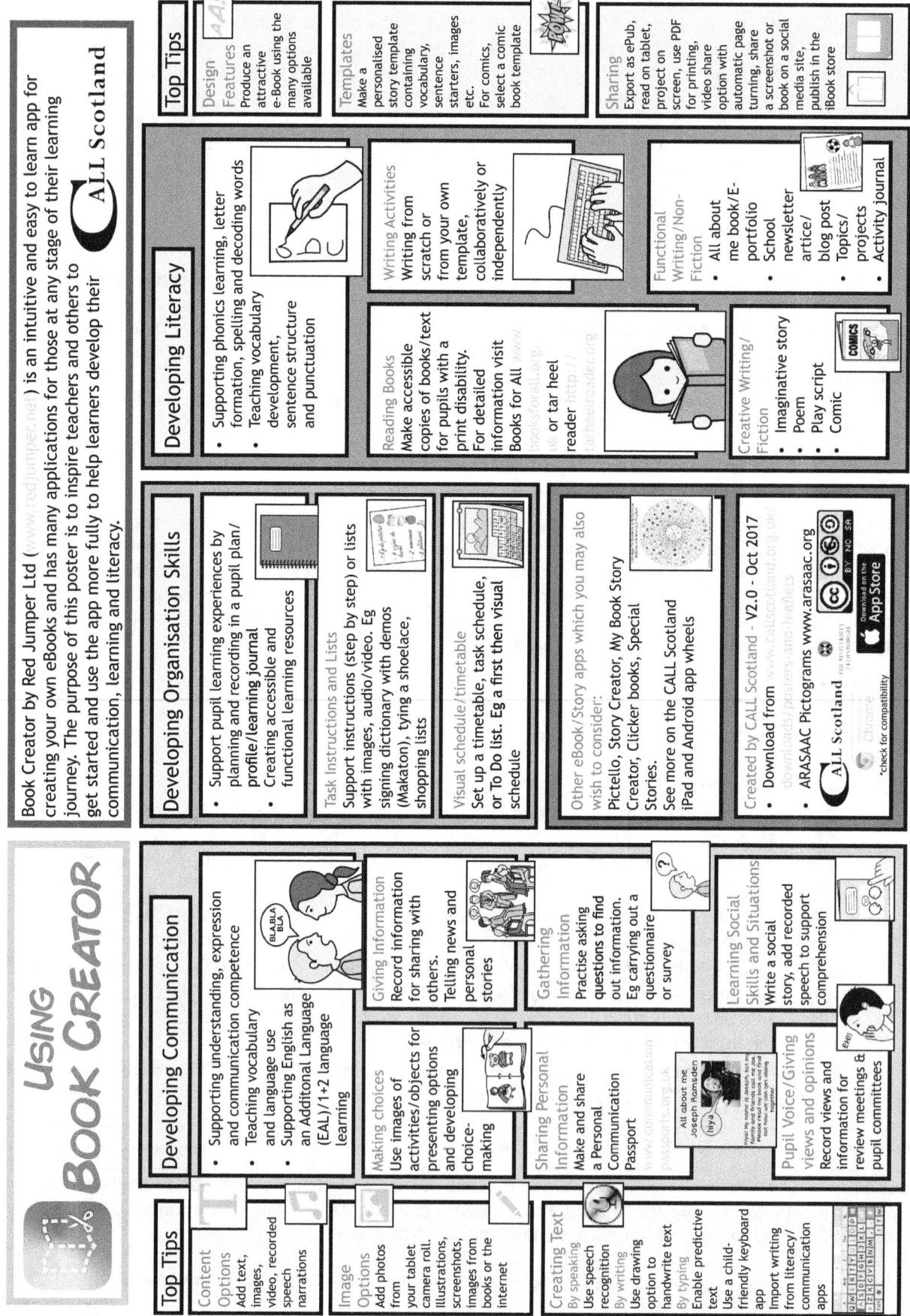

Figure 3.1 Book Creator – a tool to support ideas and ways in when making books for learners with complex needs.

- A key aspect in the use of sensory stories is that they often lead to a reduction in the vocabulary presented, but an increase in cues to the information to support long-term memory change.
- This means that learners have time and space to think about what they are learning, as there is less effort needed to process the information that is being presented to them.
- Joanna Grace has some interesting and useful training and resources to support the use of sensory stories to explore 'big ideas' such as the birth of a star (link in the following box).
- If we go back to our definition at the start of this book, we know that we are defining literacy as sharing and deriving meaning from some form of stimuli.

The question is: How does this fit into our inclusive reading framework? The learning opportunities that are provided by sensory experiences are that they enable us to support our learners to develop prediction, promote engagement, and increase attention, memory, anticipation, cooperation, and turn taking. An aim of sensory education is to create strong connections in our brain; neuron connectivity enables learners to understand and process more and more information. Sensory stories should be seen as a key aspect within an inclusive reading curriculum.

There has been a shift in the types and quality of sensory stories that are available. These stories use more than words providing sensory cues to promote consistent routines. This supports the small building blocks of learning and provides opportunities for neural pathways in the brain to join up. Following are some of the many links available, I have tried to include a mix of those that I have used an found useful.

- Check out Richard Hirstwood's training website with free and paid courses focusing on multi-sensory approaches to learning – https://hirstwood.com/ – and Richard's YouTube channel – www.youtube.com/user/richardh53 – where you can see lots of examples of supporting and creating multi-sensory activities and stories for all learners with complex needs.
- www.thesensoryprojects.co.uk/sensory – Joanna Grace has written many sensory stories that are rich in both language and sensory experiences. One of these stories, "The Birth of a Star", was written in conjunction with physicists and tells with scientific accuracy how stars are formed in stellar nurseries; it is worth checking out! As Jo says, "The Birth of a star is a very popular story that has been told in nurseries, universities, adult care settings, special and mainstream schools, literary festivals, around dinner tables and at bedsides." Find tips and guidance for creating and sharing your own sensory stories too! – www.thesensoryprojects.co.uk/guides.
- https://sensorystoriespodcast.com/inclusive-stories/ and www.helpkidzlearn.com/inclusive-stories – Watch out for one of Pete Wells' stories later in this book.
- www.rhymingmultisensorystories.com – Watch out for one of Victoria's stories later in this chapter.
- www.bagbooks.org/ – Bag Books were developed specifically for learners with SLD/PMLD and the multi-sensory approach has been adopted across the age range from babies to adults.
- www.thechildrenstrust.org.uk/sensory-stories.
- https://inclusiveteach.com/sensory-story-collection/.
- Pamis – www.pamis.org.uk – have developed their own brand of multi-sensory stories on sensitive topics, such as sexuality, transition, and growing up.

During the Jubilee, I attended a presentation where the story in the following box was shared. I was impressed by the richness of language used, and I even learnt something new about what is in the Queen's handbag! If you would like a copy of this story, Victoria has provided a link for you to access this for free.

> **Ideas in action**
>
> **The Queen's Jubilee – a multisensory adventure!**
>
> Victoria Navin
> Founder of rhyming multisensory stories
>
> **School** – Jubilee celebrations with Hebden Green Special School, Cheshire. The class group's ages ranged from EYFS to upper KS2. I adapted the story to meet the wide range of differing students' needs including PMLD, SLD, Autism, and physical development (PD).
>
> **Context** – A rhyming multi-sensory story to connect individuals, enabling them to experience the sights, sounds, and events of the Jubilee celebrations. The combination of sensory stimuli, listening to the rhyme and rhythm and their repetitive structure, supports memory and aids learning, and plays a crucial role in the development of early communication language skills.
>
> **Intent** – To provide a learning experience for all. To develop a variety of literacy skills as well as self-awareness (asking for 'more,' 'again,' and 'help.'), cause and effect, anticipation skills through the props, fine motor skills, hand-eye coordination, manipulation/control, promoting social skills (working as a group, turn taking, sharing, waiting, and listening to other students' ideas), use of mathematical language skills (colour recognition, counting, and time), role play (trying on the crown jewels), music (listening and exploring musical instruments, following instructions to 'stop' and 'go'), and more.
>
> **Implementation** – Most popular extension activity was "The Queen's Sensory Handbag". to engage the senses and promote communication skills. Language was kept simple, focusing on phrases such as 'choose' or 'take one' when presenting the bag, focusing on the name of the object, e.g., 'perfume', 'jewellery', and two-word phrases, e.g., 'silver necklace'.
>
> **Impact** – The experience created a bond between the storyteller and story explorers, enhancing and enriching experiences. It connected students to history and British culture through sensory literacy, supported communication skills (including eye contact), listening, shared attention, and language development using a total communication approach. The props were backed up by the spoken language and the use of sign language and PECS. Learners were able to make choices and sensory preferences giving the students a voice and developing their confidence, promoting a positive sense of self and celebrating achievement.
>
> **"The Queen's Jubilee" free copy** – If you would like a free copy of "The Queen's Jubilee" resource, visit the story library at https://www.rhymingmultisensorystories.com/.

When we are thinking about our environments, we need to ensure that we are providing all learners with literacy experiences so they have access to quality language opportunities. The difficulty arises when we consider the process of how we develop and gain a deeper understanding of our literacy experiences.

- We are not hard wired to learn to read; we must learn and make connections through repeated exposure to literacy.
- Due to this complex neurological and neurophysiological process, we need to enjoy words again and again to deepen our understanding.
- Learners with complex needs will need to derive meaning from representations and understand that objects, pictures, symbols, writing, and text carries meaning.
- We need to ensure that these rich experiences are accessible, meaningful, and engaging for learners with complex needs.
- We know that if we increase repetition and frequency, connections in our brains are strengthened, helping to build muscle memory.
- This will help the information to more likely be remembered and moved to the learner's long-term memory.

(Gathercole & Alloway, 2008)

Cognitive load theory promotes the importance of providing learners with access to information, via their visual and auditory pathways, to minimise overloading learners working memory (Chandler & Sweller, 1992). For learners with complex needs, we will need to consider all the senses, including movement, touch, and smell. In terms of what is known as good practice for all learners, the following key aspects should be included in an inclusive reading framework.

1. Read every day – make this part of your daily routine, ensuring that the text is language rich, fun, and engaging, with opportunities for participation and movement.
2. Use core texts as a framework to develop understanding and repeat learning. Create sensory versions, story massage versions, ebook versions, and have students create their own drama or story; write/record their own versions, and more!
3. Provide a language-rich environment and curriculum with access to multi-sensory learning opportunities.
4. Explicitly teach vocabulary in the context of great books and activities (if we want children to understand words, context is king).
5. Enable children to learn a range of stories, poems, songs, and rhymes – consider stage rather than age, making sure that you start with what interests the learner.
6. Use a variety of strategies to explore texts, including drama with access to multi-sensory and acceptable learning opportunities.
7. Access to books in many forms (e.g., digital libraries, sensory stories, feely books, sound books, audio books, drama, comics, magazines, etc.).
8. Make sure that we are all seen as readers (this includes all of the staff that work within the classroom), sharing our own likes and dislikes, making good home school links to share information and find out more about learners.

Create environments that have engaging and accessible text

The question I am often asked is how I create places for my learners to gain access to accessible experiences and text in a classroom where I may need to keep clutter to a minimum, be flexible with my space, and have some learners who may find it difficult to access traditional books. This requires us to reduce the barriers to access for learners and to use their interests and motivating texts, alongside making sure that books (in the widest sense) are durable, accessible, and fun. This supports the learning process in so many ways, most importantly by ensuring the information is given every chance to be transferred into our long-term memory (Gathercole & Alloway, 2008).

Ideas in action: case study from a special school

School – Iain Mackie, communication and interaction lead, Fairfield School, West Yorkshire.

Context – Fairfield School students have a wide range of complex needs and are aged from 4–19 years old.

Intent and Implementation – Since attending the training, I have put a real focus on ensuring that:

First, at least once a day, I or one of the members of staff in class reads a book, or a section of a book, out loud for 10 minutes. This is in addition to any sensory stories or specific intervention work we do.

Second, our school library has become part of our daily routine, with students going to the library to select a book of their choice. Depending on the students, this is either reading with them or they are given time to explore the book independently, physically interacting with the book.

Third, I have taken the approach of having a core text for our termly topic. In this term's case, it is *Princess Esme* by Joanna Grace. Everything we do in class will spring off from inspiration from this text, repeating key words or phrases throughout

> the session, and enabling us to develop a core topic vocabulary for the AAC users in my class.
>
> **Impact** – The impact of these changes was almost immediate and extremely positive. There was increased engagement and motivation. In terms of being read to after around a minute or two, all the students in class were quietly engaged in listening to the story and how I used my voice. They have heard my voice speak in ways they would not normally hear me speak and heard words they would not normally hear. All learners had greater access to literacy.

Use high-quality text as a basis for the opportunities provided

Create a reading spine for each class, key stage, interest, or school

A reading spine supports an understanding across schools about text that might be useful or engaging for learners at specific ages or interests. By providing a framework of books (in their widest sense), you ensure that there is a variety available that includes text of all types (non-fiction, poetry, drama, biographies, graphic novels, picture books, plays, rhymes, songs, etc.). There also needs to be flexibility within the reading spine or framework to add books of interest to both learners and professionals or related to themes or topics that may arise. These books should be accessible through the variety of media already discussed such as technology-based opportunities, sensory stories, story massage, and more. The important aspect is that schools have an understanding and knowledge of new, relevant, and engaging text.

> **Pie Corbett's reading spines**
>
> Pie has created some useful reading spines for each age group that contain books which are selected for specific reasons, including repetitive language and exploration of emotions or wonder, alongside the structure or format of specific books. There are many resources and lists available to support the use of engaging and interesting books for all learners. These could be arranged by topic, by age, by interest, by type – e.g., picture books or simple chapter books – and can be as vast or as limited as required. The text can be offered to learners through a variety of accessible formats.

Many of our learners may not have had the opportunity to experience the diverse and wide-ranging representations of print that exist, and therefore, they may not be aware of what interests or engages them. It is our role to provide them with opportunities to experience life and stories about other places, other people, and other times.

- Learners may have missed opportunities to visualise themselves as central characters due to the lack of representation of learners with complex needs in stories.
- There is a growing list of accessible text which have a more inclusive set up involving the story and characters (e.g., www.goodreads.com/genres/inclusive-books).
- Our classrooms must contain text which our learners will read. If they are unable to access it, if it is not engaging, or if there are other reasons for it not being something that they would like to look at, there is no point to it being in the classroom.
- Classrooms should have books which range from easy to increasing difficulty.
- Learners should have access to decodable books, whereby skills learnt can be practised and confidence built.
- We need to look for books that are all shaped differently, coloured differently, and created in ways that will provide the learner with as much multi-sensory experience as possible.

> **Ideas in action: examples from a special school**
>
> **School** – Ceanna MacGregor, principal teacher, Greenburn School, East Kilbride.
>
> **Impact** – After the literacy lessons training, I realised the value of adding text to non-text sensory stories.

By using an agreed list of books across our schools that might be interesting, engaging, or motivating, we open the world of literacy for all learners. Once we have a shared understanding of the importance of a wide range of books and topics, we can use established good practice (sensory story format, story massage, immersive story experiences) to provide deeper, more engaging experiences for all learners. The key is to provide opportunities for us to repeat, repeat, and repeat with consistency, alongside the opportunity for learners to read (in the widest sense) and experience the same text and language, again and again.

Create collections using a variety of different types of texts

Around 90% of our vocabulary is only encountered in reading and not in speech. It is important to make sure that the environment includes a range of genres, topics, and types of narrative, with error free access to build up confidence. Simon Smith has been influential in my choice of text to recommend during my training and support for schools. I follow him on Twitter (@smithsmm) and I really enjoy the picture book recommendations that he provides at https://smithsmm.wordpress.com/.

I have created the following list of some of the main ingredients of a rich literacy environment (should be included but are not exclusive).

- **Wordless/picture books** – Lists of these which are relevant for older learners, too (e.g., Books Beyond Words at www.booksbeyondwords.co.uk), use pictures to tell stories that engage and empower people with learning difficulties on topics that are of social or health importance, such as death and dying or crime. The illustrations are developed through consultation with adults with learning difficulties, and although there are suggestions for words to use, the books are essentially pictures only.
- **Repetitive texts** – Can take many forms from questions and answers, predictive patterns, cumulative sequencing, repeated last line, and more. These build confidence, interest, and engagement for learners. It is important to remember that the learners' interests should guide our choices and then we can provide an expanded selection of books. It may be that the interest is one which is too young for the learner, but we need to remember to focus on stage rather than age, using their interest in something such as *Thomas the Tank Engine* as a way in to build up other books/texts based on this format.
- **Alphabet books** – Alphabet books using engaging formats, freezes, or alphabet arcs. Use books that will encourage it understanding within older readers
- **Fiction and non-fiction** – Instructions, recipes, focusing on nature, and science as well as fiction.
- **Plays** – Such as Julia Donaldson's "Plays to Read" and "Plays to Act" – are crucial to develop communication, empathy (understanding ourselves and others), building fluency, building vocabulary, and enhancing comprehension.
- **Comics and graphic novels**.
- **Compact discs, story books, or audio tapes**.
- **Decodable text** – Provide opportunities to consolidate, practice, and repeat learning, making it active (www.phonicsbooks.com).
- **Social media opportunities** – Explore pages related to their interests.
- **Digital media opportunities** – Emails and texts.
- **Own-made books**.

- **Sensory stories, bag books, story massage, story mats, story boards**.
- **Reference books** – Encyclopaedias, dictionaries.
- **Digital libraries**.
- **Augmented reality texts**.
- **Pop-up books (my favourite)**.

Accessibility

The key role played by accessibility has been discussed throughout this chapter and is something that needs to be remembered and considered throughout the rest of this book. I have spent time collaborating with schools, colleges, publishers, Trusts/MATs, and families, looking at how to support the development of reading for all learners. The focus will often begin with: What do we need to buy, create, provide, or get in terms of resources, books, or knowledge? I always begin with supporting people to look at what is currently provided, the impact of this for all learners, and if there are any barriers to access. If learners cannot access this environment or the resources that are contained within it, then there is no point in it being in place.

There are many areas of difficulties when it comes to accessing literacy activities for learners with complex needs and those with significant needs. These may relate to muscular problems, sensory issues, executive function impairments and more. Teaching experiences require planning for access for all learners to achieve and consider how they will access learning. For example, ensure opportunities for non-verbal learners to indicate choice and move on (yes/no cards, same, different cards, iPad, AAC, eye gaze, E-Tran frame, switch, pointer).

Use low-tech accessibility to support physical mobility and fine motor issues (page turners, gaps to separate pages, book slopes, laminate pages, plastic sheets and ring binders, rubber finger cots/headsticks/hand splints on tips to aid traction, coloured pages, fonts, and more). Use assistive technology, speech activated devices, AAC, switches, or joysticks to select the next sound in a pattern, hear sound, select card, turn page, select book, or read independently.

Ideas in action: case study from a special school

School – Rebekah Clee, Fairfield School, West Yorkshire.

Context – Fairfield School students have a wide range of complex needs and are aged from 4–19 years old.

Intent – The focus was to see how we could make books more accessible. The case study took time, as I spent time with many different students in school, those with vision and cerebral visual impairment (CVI) needs, physical needs, and those who may not be used to turning pages as part of reading. I looked at what ways we can change books, making reading a task without barriers. We wanted reading to be fun and engaging, and we wanted to make it possible for pupils to enjoy reading independently.

Implementation – My observations showed books were hard to access for the students. The pupils often turned the whole book round or would pull at the pages; other pupils turned numerous pages at once, meaning they were not reading the story correctly (Figure 3.2). I also observed that when pupils were handling books, staff would often need to intervene to enable a pupil to turn a page or would even at times turn the pages for them. The main issue is that some pupils were frustrated in their handling of books and this took away the enjoyment or made the task a challenge.

Figure 3.2 Pupil having difficulty turning page.

When the pages were turned, it was often several together. This caused her to feel frustrated and although she was happy to handle the book, it did however mean that books could not be enjoyed independently. The observation also showed the book was handled for only a short time and often, the pupil did not engage in the activity; the initial curiosity was quickly forgotten.

Figure 3.3 Pupil selecting with colours and textures to use.

Pupils were involved in exploring materials and colours that they would use if they were making their own book or adding to a book (Figure 3.3). Enabling pupils to feel and touch helped to show what colours and feelings engaged them further. It also enabled me to explore the colours that were more accessible for pupils with vision needs such as bright colours on dark items, or yellows and reds for pupils with CVI.

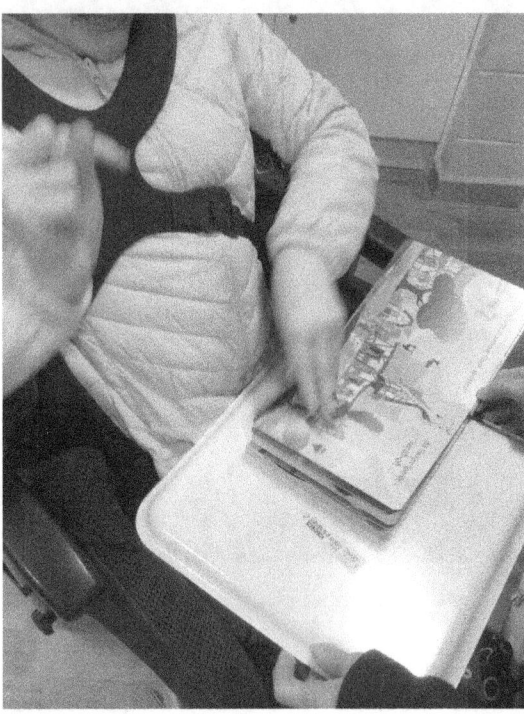

Figure 3.4 Pupil trying out pom pom as a page turner.

The adaptations included adding different items to the books to aid turning the pages. In some books, we added coloured items that supported vision needs. The first item we added was pom poms (Figure 3.4). The pom poms were stuck onto each page, and this created enough separation between the pages to enable the book to be accessible. The book where we added lollipop sticks (Figure 3.5) was a huge success, as the lollipop sticks enabled an easy to grasp handle.

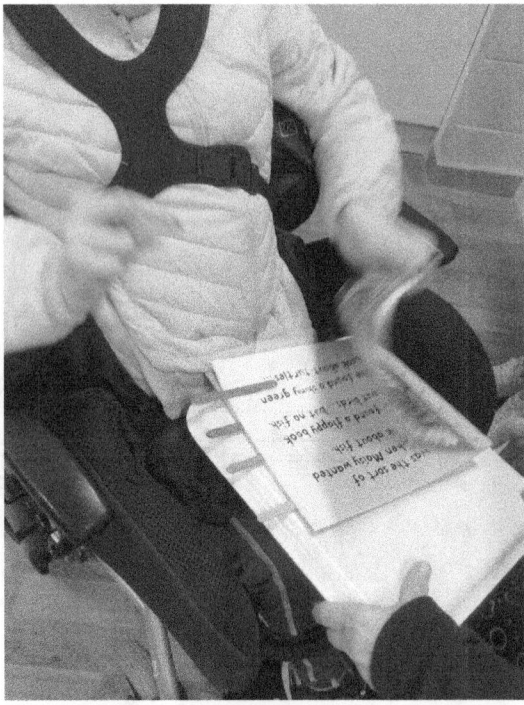

Figure 3.5 Lollipop stick page turners were a success.

> **Impact** – The initial observations and the changes made a difference to the way many pupils accessed books. The changes were simple but took away barriers and enabled more independence over the reading experience. The Teach Us Too course opened my eyes to the importance of looking and challenging reading barriers for all learners.

Create digital libraries for learners

Accessibility is provided from the start for all learners using rich and engaging digital libraries. Universal design for learning is a framework or approach that starts with the understanding that if you begin with an inclusive view that considers the needs of everyone from the start, you reduce the need for any changes or adaptations.

> *The goal of Universal Design Learning (UDL) is to use a variety of teaching methods to remove any barriers to learning. It is about building in flexibility that can be adjusted for every person's strengths and needs!*
>
> (Understood, 2022)

This means that you consider how to make things accessible from the start for all learners. Creating digital libraries provides ways for all learners to access text, through listening, seeing, and participating in immersive literacy experiences. This provides learners with every opportunity to develop literacy by ensuring repeated exposure to text. It is part of the UK Equality Act (2021) that all schools must ensure that their local authority makes reasonable adjustments to ensure all texts are accessible to all learners. There are many online and free resources available, as well as subscriptions to different organisations to provide text. A practical guide from a useful organisation, CALL Scotland (Figure 3.6), provides an overview of some of the ways that digital libraries support all learners to access text.

Many of these libraries contain accessible, multi-sensory experiences to bring literacy to life. Following is a list of *some* of the accessible online book collections that are out there.

- RNIB Education Collection – www.rnib.org.uk/reading-services/rnib-bookshare
- www.tarheelreader.org – A digital collection of free books that you can add to and find out who has read your book and where in the world they may be
- www.childrenslibrary.org – An international children's list of books by many different categories including different languages, topics, genres, etc.
- www.watchknowlearn.org – A free American resource
- www.bookshare.org
- https://livingpaintings.org/ – A free library of tactile books with audio description
- www.storylineonline.net
- www.Kidsread2kids
- Free eBook library – Practice reading with phonics eBooks (Oxford Owl)
- www.Storynory.com
- www.acessablebookcollection.org
- www.tumblebooks.com
- www.HelpKidzLearn.com/shop
- https://sensorystoriespodcast.com/inclusive-stories/
- Local libraries have access to their own digital collections

Assistive technology

Assistive technology at the start of my career consisted of using the video player on a weekly basis to share, Look and Read episodes with my learners! Assistive technology has a huge

46 *The importance of accessible literacy-rich environments*

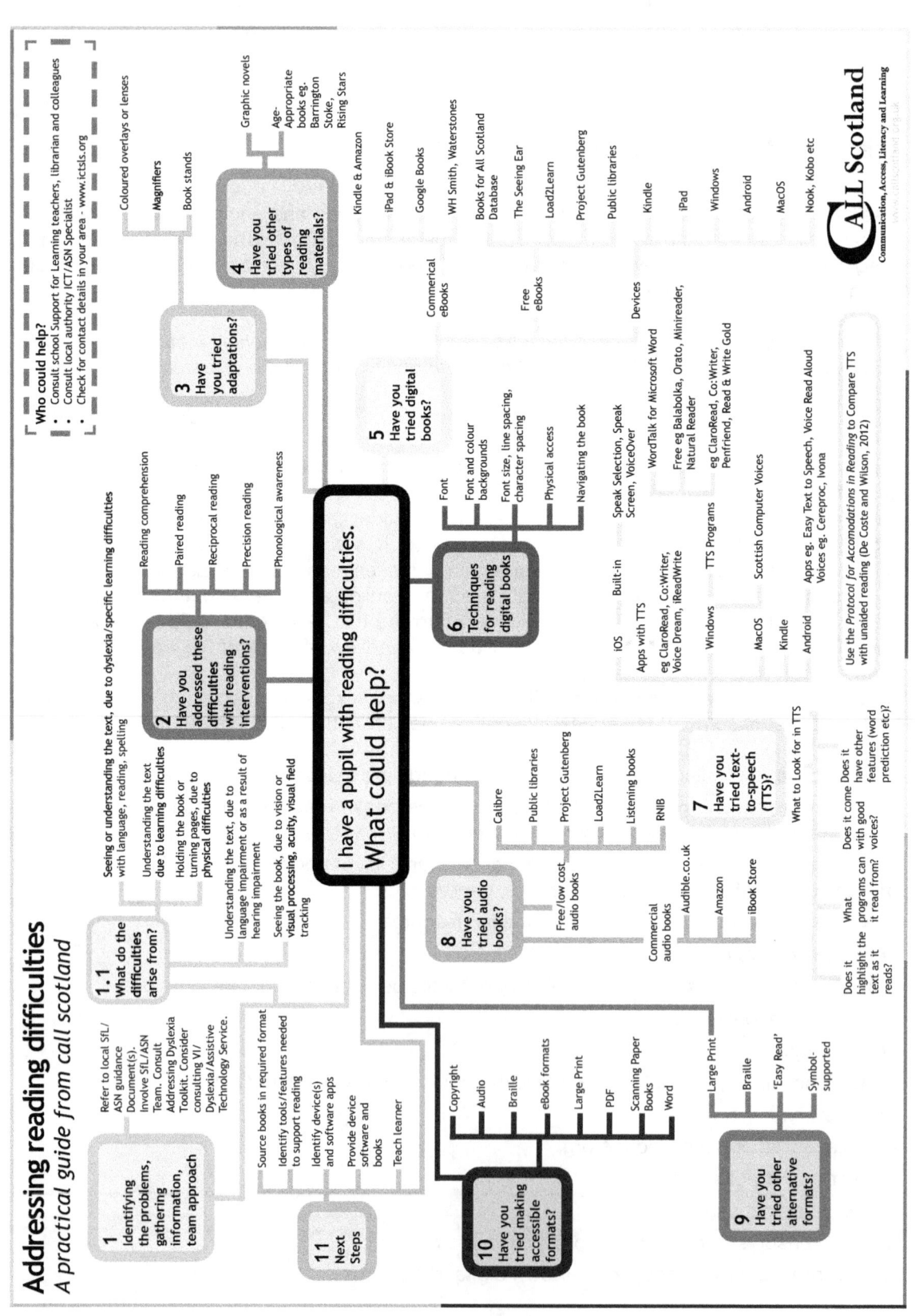

Figure 3.6 CALL Scotland addressing reading difficulties guide.

role to play in the teaching of reading for all students, but particularly those with complex learning needs. The key is that we understand why we are using it and how it will support access for all learners. Therefore, prior to any assistive technology being used, it is important that all professionals understand what they are trying to achieve. Too often, it is the importance of ensuring that the activity is accessible that may halt or prevent the learner from participating. Assistive technology should be inclusively available as part of a universal design for learning, which means that it is there when learners need it.

I have been lucky to have the opportunity to work with some extremely passionate and knowledgeable professionals within this area. Listening to Carol Allen present on anything connected to literacy and assistive technology is a joy. One of the quotes from Carol that I found particularly influential in my current practice is, "Lives are changed by assistive technology. Please keep trying and give it time" (Allen, 2020).

The emphasis should be on what the learner needs to reduce barriers to learning, and therefore how assistive technology can support this. This also means that when assistive technology is used as part of a lesson, it is not seen as something different or special. This leads to a more inclusive culture within schools and classrooms, therefore supporting more learners to be part of all sessions.

> **Provide tools that enable learners to explore and access books in many ways**
>
> All smart devices (Alexa, etc)., and technology (Kindles, iPads, and other screens with loaded programmes using augmented reality).
>
> Portable text readers (scanning pens, www.scanningpens.com, has a useful free literacy passport to download) take the difficulties out of independent reading and keeps readers focused on task.
>
> Systems to mount books, devices to ensure they are in position that learners can access, seating systems and variations, stand-up seating or desks.
>
> Communication aids, symbol cards, Picture Exchange Communication System (PECS), and communication books.
>
> Eye gaze access (consider low tech opportunities using E-tran frames), Switch access.
>
> Opportunities to make choices using pre or non-verbal communication strategies, armbands (yes/no), pointers add more.
>
> EBook apps (scholastic story', a story before bed, tales2go).
>
> Read aloud options (consider digital screenwriters, or book sovereign could recorded or uploaded on YouTube, or text-to-speech read options that are free on many sites) A useful app that learners can read too is www.fonetti.com/.
>
> Audio (BBC school radio, EYFS, listen and play, BBC CBeebies).
>
> Audible apps/tools on all programmes.

As the world of technology and innovation develops, the list of accessible support is growing for us all.

> **My experience**
>
> If you look at the availability of assistive technology on our devices, within apps and on our computers, it is now inbuilt and easily/freely available. Features such as text to speech or speech to text are used by many of us at different times and within different tasks. During the process of writing this book, I began to suffer with arthritis in my wrist due to the amount of time that I have spent working on the computer typing. I purchased a stand-up mouse which revolutionised my typing, and an adapted keyboard to support my posture. Both adaptations were useful, but I still found it painful to type. I began to explore options that enabled me to use speech to control my computer, and finally began to rely on speech-to-text software. In fact, much of this book was written using speech-to-text technology, and I may never go back to purely typing. We need to say less with simple, clear, repetitive instructions.

Call Scotland have developed many useful infographics, Figure 3.7 provides an overview of inclusive learning resources.

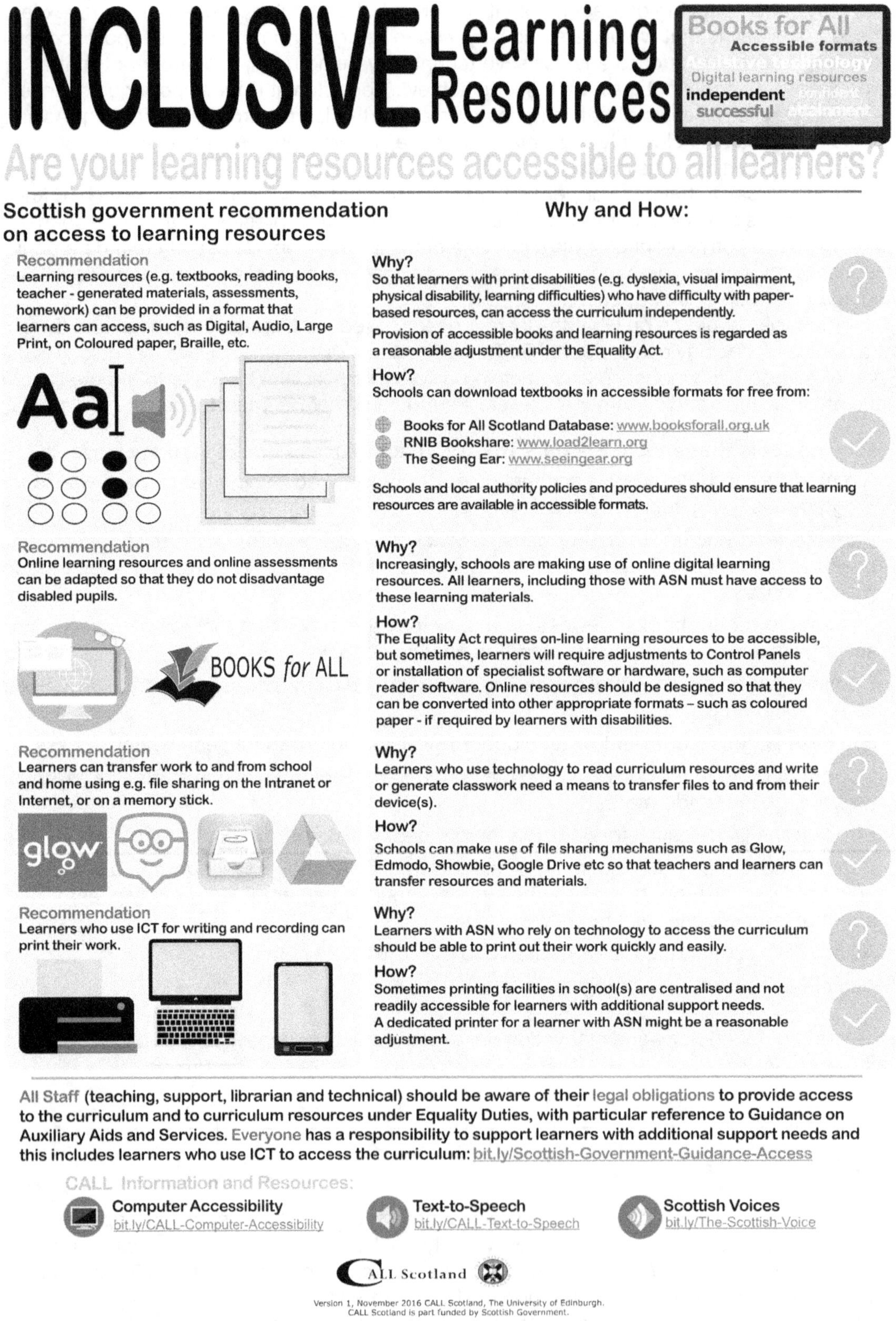

Figure 3.7 CALL Scotland's overview of inclusive learning resources.

Technology can be used in many ways to support learners with complex needs in literacy including

- Making books, texts, websites, and digital content accessible (read aloud, larger print, digital, accessible by switches/eye gaze, and more)
- Provides text to speech and/or speech to text to gain extra visual information or increase learning about sight words and sounds
- Supporting executive function difficulties (recording information, organising, structuring).

There is a wealth of accessible functions on iPads/iPhones that can support using our voice to activate all aspects and all parts of the programme. Immersive reader within Microsoft products enables all aspects of text to be accessible to all learners. Using a computer or tablet provides many supportive assistive features that are not possible with paper-based activities such as handwriting or reading printed text such as spelling support (writing) or text to speech (reading). To make experiences as accessible as possible consider the importance of ensuring all learners have access to:

- Trained staff and volunteers
- Communication partners
- High- and low-technology assistive devices
- Texts as wide-ranging as you can make them, featuring books in their widest sense
- Provide objects, sensory stimuli, areas, puppets, displays, freezes, table-top resources, etc.

Create and share language and text across the school

Make the most of spaces and places across our environment, considering inside and outside areas. Using outside learning environments will be hugely motivating for many learners. Consider creating story trails, word searches, scavenger hunts, and using some of the areas where a learner is most likely to spend time. Our corridors are huge spaces where learners spend time that can have visual sounds, pictures, sound tiles, and games as they go around the school. Any approach to the teaching of reading must include a consideration of the development of language, vocabulary, and how well all learners will get the chance to extend and increase their vocabularies. At the heart is the importance of creating a curiosity and love of words and vocabulary for all learners. We need to look at how we can incorporate interesting, unusual, and engaging language across our day or week.

> **My experience**
>
> When I think about my son at the age of 3 when we went to the local library, he did not want to engage or look at the books contained within the children's section. At the time, I was looking for a murder mystery book myself which I would often read whilst he was playing. My son instead headed towards the thick books in the adult section. He then selected one of the biggest and heaviest books he could find and gave it to me for him to take home. I realised that his experience of books had been from watching me and therefore he wanted to model and copy my reading behaviour. This book then remained with him every time we went out; he would spend time holding it, flicking the pages and telling everyone he was "doing reading".

Think about where learners will read

Inspiring classrooms are crucial for any learner. Learners with complex needs require a greater amount of thought in order to minimise barriers to learning, maximise engagement and consider how the classroom enables the offer of rich multi-sensory learning experiences. For our pre-formal learners, we need to consider how we are using our space to enable learners time to respond, to support the use of routines and ensuring that the environment is flexible to enable focus on the activity being offered. We need to consider how to support learners with moving on to activities that involve increasing shared attention.

- Make comfortable reading areas both inside and out.
- Make the most of the many different environments that we have around us where learners can explore and experience the world of literacy.
- Consider how we read and where we are comfortable, and therefore use the many imaginative ideas that people have for reading areas, reading boxes, reading activities, reading trolleys, and looking at maybe using tents and dipping into reading in a comfortable area, creating different kinds of seating or accessible areas.
- Importantly, make sure it is built into every day.

50 *The importance of accessible literacy-rich environments*

> **Ideas in action: case study from a special school**
>
> **School** – Bex Watton, Early years foundation stage (Eyfs) teacher, Linden Lodge School, London.
>
> **Context** – Linden Lodge School is a day and residential regional school for pupils with vision impairment. It caters for learners aged 2–19 with vision impairment, hearing impairment, and multi-sensory impairment.
>
> **Intent** – Supporting the importance of rich experiences; in this case, a book corner. To provide my learners with a reading-rich environment where they can enjoy reading in all forms and access it on a level that is appropriate and engaging for them. Classrooms can have attractive and inviting zones and still be a safe and comfortable environment for the learners.
>
> **Implementation** – Teaching children with ASC, I find that classrooms are thought of as being plain and bare to avoid being a distracting and overwhelming environment if done correctly. I introduce the children in groups/whole class to the story and the props on Monday and revisit it Wednesday and Friday. On Tuesday and Thursday, children spend time in the book corner one-to-one with an adult to share a reading experience – this can be rereading the story of the week; sharing favourite stories, rhymes, or songs; or exploring different motivating texts. Throughout the week during continuous provision, children access the book corner and explore the props and books independently; retell stories in small groups; read a variety of symbols, pictures, and/or text; and enjoy reading.
>
> **Impact** – My learners love this space! We enjoy multi-sensory storytelling experiences in this area and story massage. This is impacted on their opportunities to be engaged and participate in stories and print enabling a greater degree of independent choice and ultimately reading.
>
> (To find out more about story massage, follow this link www.storymassage.co.uk/)

As discussed throughout this book, we need to widen our definition of a book. With the advances in technology we all access text in so many ways, I love these sensory umbrellas from Richard Hirstwood, that capture a story in a multi-sensory way (Figure 3.8).

Figure 3.8 A story umbrella by Richard Hirstwood.

When you get the accessibility, environment and expectations right, learning has no limits, as illustrated in the following real-life example.

> ### Ideas in action: case study from a special school
>
> **Context** – This pupil, Sarah, is an eye gaze user and has engaged really well in literacy instruction. Previously, Sarah really enjoyed books and listening to stories, and we would model words and sentences on her device from the story.
>
> **Intent** – Implementation of five emergent literacy practices as outlined in *Comprehensive Literacy for All* (Koppenhaver & Erickson). How one particular pupil's literacy experience has changed as a result of this.
>
> **Implementation** – Sarah has been engaged in phonics and alphabet awareness. We have been covering a letter a day in class and she has responded really well to this. She sometimes finds the letter she is learning about that day on her keyboard page and often finds words on her communication pages starting with that letter. One of the LCAs created flashcards for each letter that are personalised for Sarah to include items and characters she particularly likes. This has helped to engage her in alphabet awareness lessons. Sarah has had opportunities to engage in predictable chart writing activities too.
>
> **Impact** – Now, she is encouraged to think about and respond to what she is being read. She likes using her communication device to speak about what she thinks might happen next, where a character is going, or what character/animal is going to be in the story. She is generally more engaged and interested in books and has an opportunity to respond to what she is reading.
>
> She has several times said "pen" on her eye gaze device when I get the pen out to start writing! She has contributed her own ideas during these sessions – not always words that were expected, but they are her ideas. For example, when we were writing a chart about what clothes we wear in winter, Sarah's sentence was "I put on sunglasses"! We spoke about how sometimes it can be sunny in winter and we need sunglasses. This week, our chart was about the Queen, in the leadup to the Jubilee celebrations. Sarah's sentence was "The Queen is clean"! Not something we had talked about previously but I am sure she is right. It has been great to see Sarah's progress so far, and I am sure she will continue to make progress in literacy in the future.
>
> Iona Maltman

Provide real opportunities to bring literacy to life

It is crucial that experiences of text are embedded into real-life opportunities to hear, see, and be part of rich literacy experiences that can be provided from watching a performance or a drama.

- Experiences that can be provided through being part of a choir, where you can hear and feel and be part of an environment full of sound.
- Providing opportunities to be part of an orchestra, again considering this in the widest sense, using technology, digital resources, apps, and instruments to bring literacy experiences to life.
- When we are exploring language, some of the most engaging opportunities for this to happen are performing or being part of something whereby you are listening or playing with sounds related to text, songs, stories, limericks, tongue twisters, alphabet rhymes, and more.

> ### Time for reflection
>
> Consider how you use technology to make life more accessible (I use speech to text to minimise repetitive strain injury, and I also use magnified font on my phone due to my failing eyes!).
> Now think of a learner in your classroom and how they might benefit from increased accessibility to support the development and inclusion within a reading framework.

References

Allen, C. (2020) Assistive technology for all using ambitious teaching. *Proceedings of the British Assistive Technology Association Conference* [online], November 19.

Britton, J. (1972) Language and learning. *British Journal of Educational Studies*, 20, (2), pp. 245–246.

Chandler, P. & Sweller, J. (1992) The split-attention effect as a factor in the design of instruction. *Psychology British Journal of Educational Psychology*, 62, (2), pp. 233–246 [online] Available at: https://psycnet.apa.org/record/1992-41746-001 [Accessed: 14/07/2022]

Department for Education. (2021) *The reading framework: Teaching the foundations of literacy* [online] Available at: www.gov.uk/government/publications/the-reading-framework-teaching-the-foundations-of-literacy [Accessed: 23/06/2022]

Gathercole, S. & Alloway, T.P. (2008) *Working Memory and Learning: A Practical Guide for Teachers*. London: Paul Chapman Publishing.

1Equality Act. (2010) *Guidance* [online] Available at: https://www.gov.uk/guidance/equality-act-2010-guidance#:~:text=The%20Equality%20Act%202010%20legally,strengthening%20protection%20in%20some%20situations

Grove, N. (2022) *Storytelling, Special Needs and Disabilities: Practical Approaches for Children and Adults*. London: Routledge.

Heath, S.B. (1983) Research currents: A lot of talk about nothing. *Language Arts*, 60, (8), pp. 999–1007 [online] Available at: www.jstor.org/stable/41961563 [Accessed: 13/07/2022]

Koppenhaver, D. & Erickson, K. (2020) *Comprehensive Literacy for All: Teaching Students with Significant Disabilities to Read and Write*. Paul H. Brookes Publishing Co.

Myatt, M. (2020) *Using stories in the curriculum* [online] Available at: www.marymyatt.com/blog/using-stories-in-the-curriculum [Accessed: 03/05/2022]

Understood. (2022) *What is universal design for learning?* [online] Available at: www.understood.org/en/articles/universal-design-for-learning-what-it-is-and-how-it-works [Accessed: 24/06/2022]

4 How does reading develop?

In this chapter, I will provide a brief overview of how we learn to read. This will be discussed alongside real-life examples and illustrations to support greater clarity. I will discuss the development of reading in terms of the models that are embedded into today's literacy curriculum based on the 'Simple View of Reading' (word recognition and language comprehension) (Gough & Tunmer, 1986) alongside Scarborough's 'Reading Rope' (Scarborough, 2001). This will be placed within a context of ensuring learning is accessible for all. As emphasised by Such (2021), it is one thing to be *told* why something works; it is another thing entirely to *understand* why something works.

To understand how to teach reading to all learners, we need a clear understanding of how reading develops. We must understand the why to ensure we use all the approaches and strategies available to support gaps, barriers, and strengthen skills for all learners. By strengthening our understanding around the mechanics of learning to read, we can use existing knowledge, strategies, and practice to remove the barriers to learning that may exist for learners with complex needs and ensure effective support is in place to support them. By understanding processes involved in the development of reading among typically developing learners, we may understand more about why reading problems exist and how we might teach (Snowling & Hume, 2006). This enables us to explore some of the ways for learners with complex needs and be aware of why these strategies are important in terms of the teaching of reading. We need to be clear about what we are doing and why this is our intent (Ofsted, 2019).

Learning to read is a difficult skill to develop; unlike learning to speak, we need to be taught skills. The process is not something that is linear, whereby one thing is learnt and then the next. Difficulties in learning these skills will present in many ways and require an understanding about why specific aspects are key to the development of the process. To support learners with difficulties, we need to be aware of skills that may be missing and provide opportunities to develop these. We need to strengthen and learn these skills to support areas that may be impaired or impossible to develop. In terms of learning to read, there is no simple process whereby one thing is learnt and then the next. Unlike learning to speak, which appears to require no direct teaching, the complex task of learning to read has been described as the one of the most important learning challenges faced in the first years of education (Muter, 2003).

The human brain was built for oral communication rather than reading; the brain will often prioritise auditory information and has a much bigger capacity for this than for visual information. Kuhl's influential research (Kuhl, 2011; Zhao & Kuhl, 2017) around the development of communication in babies emphasises the importance of interactions to engage the social brain. Language is learnt through meaningful interactions with others and being immersed in language-rich experiences. It is through relationships with caregivers that the differences between sounds is understood, learnt, and discriminated against. This leads to the creation of sound maps and neural pathways.

Reading is something that has evolved as a requirement once language becomes written down. These early experiences contribute to the foundation skills that are required. The neuroplasticity of the brain's connections and circuits link and change in response to interactions with the environment (Wolf, 2017). The environments therefore need to provide experiences of language and opportunities to tune into this language, to build the foundation required for the development of attention, cognition, memory, language/literacy, and sensory and motor skills that the learner needs.

> **Ideas in action: case study from a special school**
>
> **School** – Mrs Connacher, principal teacher, Croftcroighn School, Glasgow.
>
> **Context** – Croftcroighn Primary School is purpose-built to meet the needs of children with complex additional support needs, including cognitive, sensory, communication and physical impairments from P1–P7. The school also has a nursery which admits children from the age of 2 years. There are currently 61 pupils attending the school.

> This pupil is 6 years old and his main modes of communication are body language, vocalisation, and a few words such as "no".
>
> **Intent** – Using photographs and creating personalised photobooks to support engagement.
>
> **Implementation** – I produced class journals using photographs taken during the term. There was a short piece of text at the bottom of each page where the pupils in the photos were named, with a brief description of where they were or what the activity was. I printed one for each pupil to send home to provide opportunities for all pupils to share in a reading experience with their families.
>
> **Impact** – When I brought them into class, he recognised the cover and ran over to me to take one, turned it the correct way up and sat on the floor to look through it. These actions demonstrated many skills that we were not aware that he had and were another reminder not to underestimate the abilities of our pupils. His mum reported back that he really enjoyed reading his book at home as well. He has also recently called her "Mum" for the first time, too. It was amazing to see the way he took ownership of the book, turning the pages and naming his peers with no prompting or direction from an adult. He was reading for pleasure!

Literacy is a process that begins at birth, with skills and knowledge developing concurrently and interrelatedly. For learners with complex needs, this will be a very different journey, and it therefore requires appropriate and supportive planning. Adams emphasises that reading should not be viewed as a "unitary skill", but as a "complex system of skills and knowledge" (Adams, 1990, p. 3). When we are thinking about the teaching of reading to all learners, including those with complex needs, it is important that we follow the science. There have been many developments in the scientific research into how we learn to read, and there has been much information provided about aspects that are important to this. Is our role to use our knowledge and understanding to shape the experiences and opportunities that we offer our learners.

The science of reading

Developments in research relating to reading and a greater awareness of the science of reading have led to a reading revolution. There has been a shift in thinking in terms of reading development for all learners, moving towards the evidence from cognitive psychology and neuroscience research views of the 'science of reading' – the focus being a greater emphasis on the importance of teaching phonics and systematic instruction as key aspects in teaching reading. The science of reading is an accumulated body of research that has been built up over many years; it forms the basis of what has been referred to as the "Reading Wars" (Castles et al., 2018).

How to best teach reading is one of the most controversial topics in education. In special education, this debate has been ongoing and led to differences in approach and strategies used. In mainstream education, the focus had been on whether early instruction should focus letter-to-sound correspondences so that children can learn to sound out words (systematic phonics) or focus on the meanings of written words embedded in stories (whole language). Much of this debate has provided educators with an increase in information around how children and young people learn to read, but it does not provide all the answers. As Such states, "what research into reading does provide is the basis through which we can make informed decisions" (Such, 2021, p. 128)

Within special education this debate is greatly complicated by another dimension concerning the appropriateness of the teaching of reading for some of the learners. The publication of the reading framework provided some clarity around expectations for the teaching of reading to all learners including those with complex needs (DfE, 2021). Research by Dehaene (2009) concludes,

> It is simply not true that there are hundreds of ways to learn to read. Every child is unique . . . but when it comes to reading we all have roughly the same brain that imposes the same constraints and the same learning sequence.

Evidence suggests that most children with moderate to severe and complex needs are not 'visual learners', as previously thought (DfE, 2021). If we look at some of the statistics that are presented within the reading framework, it emphasises that a comparatively small number of children and young people who have profound and multiple learning difficulties (PMLD), sensory (hearing and visual), and/or multi-sensory impairments (MSI) and may be unable to access aspects of the reading framework. Ann Sullivan (2020) has produced her own phonics for special education needs (SEN) scheme and illustrates a breakdown in Figure 4.1.

According to DfE census data, January 2020, 0.001% can be described as unable to access a structured approach in some way (DfE, 2020). Some, but not all, of this group of children may be working at the equivalent of a very early developmental stage.

As discussed previously, some professionals consider that for these pupils, time is best spent working on communication, interaction, and other key areas of development. With the agreement of families, it may be the case that literacy does not form part of the curriculum for these learners. As with any decision that is made, there needs to be a clear rationale for this, and this needs to be revised and discussed on a regular basis. We need to ensure that opportunities for learners to engage in rich literacy opportunities are presented whenever this might be relevant for them. It is important to consider the difficulties that exist in terms of conducting research in this area, and specifically with learners who have the most significant complex needs. There is a long-overdue movement focusing on the importance of involving all learners in the information gathering and research processes that take place to ensure that they are fully consented participants.

As I discussed in Chapter 3, we need to consider if the barrier to the teaching of reading is us, as opposed to our learners. I have recently been involved in discussions with Pie Corbett, who raised a very interesting point, suggesting that special schools are where mainstream schools were 15 years ago. At that time, the use of phonics as a regular structured approach would have been questioned and dismissed. If you go into a mainstream primary school now, there will be no discussion about whether phonics teaching should be used for learners, as it is clearly established as an important means and part of reading instruction for all children. In fact, the discussions that are happening now are around how best to support and teach learners within secondary mainstream schools the mechanics of phonics.

There are some interesting discussions around how to ensure accessible, appropriate, and relevant approaches are in place to support older typically developing learners and to support

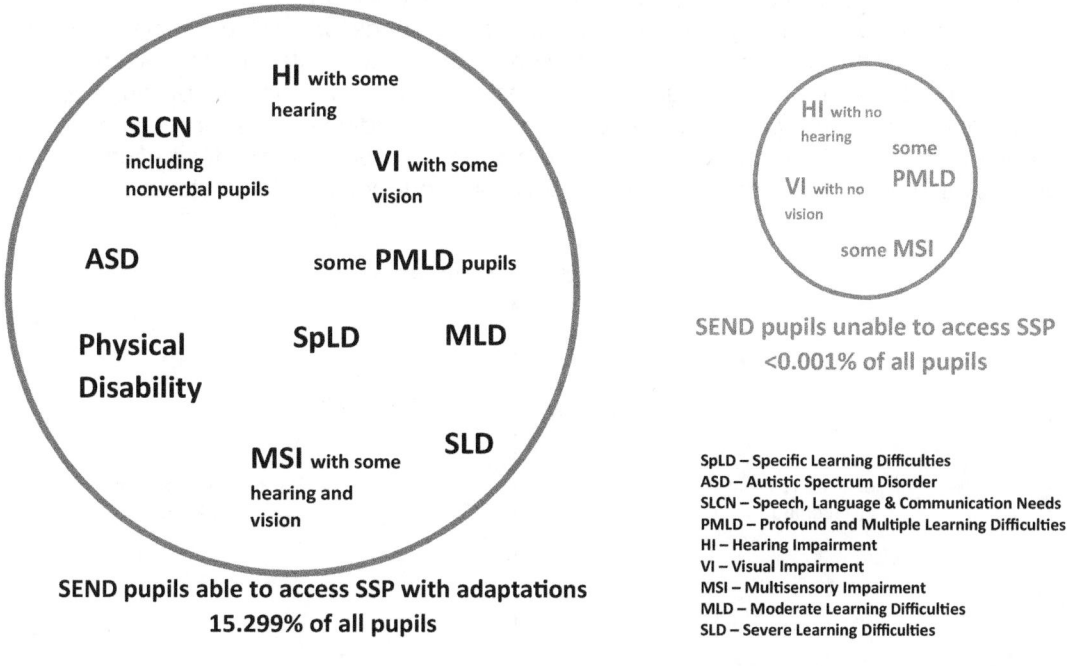

Figure 4.1 SEND pupils and breakdown in terms of learning to read using a structured approach by Ann Sullivan.

staff to ensure a greater understanding of how we learn to read. It may be that discussions that we are having within special education around the applicability of a structured synthetic phonics-based approach for learners with complex needs may not be so polarised in the future. "The EEF considers phonics to be one of the most secure and best-evidenced areas of pedagogy and recommends all schools use a systematic approach to teaching it" (DfE, 2021, p. 6).

> **My experience**
>
> My experience of teacher training college consisted of an afternoon session on the teaching of reading which was aimed at learners who are typically developing. I was then placed with a class of 32 Year 2 learners, many of whom struggled with reading. I was lost! A major concern was that many of the children did not want to read or take part in activities; my initial worry was that I could not make a child read. Where should I begin? I was amazed at the gaps in my knowledge – and when I began teaching in mainstream and special needs schools, I found out that this was true for many staff. There is lots of information available, but it can seem complicated and hard to use. When I reflect back on this experience some 30 years later, and the questions that I am asked during my consultancy work, I am aware that these gaps still exist for all professionals. Learning to read is a complex process and one which we are learning more about each day. Without the appropriate professional development, it will be hard to move forward and consider what are the right opportunities that we should be providing for all learners including those with complex needs. Before we consider how to teach reading to learners with complex needs, we need to understand how it develops.

How does reading develop?

Research focusing on the development of reading has aimed to provide insight into the cognitive processes involved in learning to read by using models of typically developing and skilled readers as a framework. Psychologists have tried to simplify this investigation by focusing on the observation of two simple, yet essential, components needed to become a skilled reader: language comprehension and word recognition (Stuart, 2006). The Rose Review advocated the model proposed by the Simple View of Reading (Gough & Tunmer, 1986) and this is embedded into current UK practice. According to this framework, reading comprises of two dimensions of printed word recognition and language comprehension (Such, 2021).

Word recognition refers to the ability to recognise words presented in and out of context, either by sight or through decoding/blending phonemes (the smallest units of sound heard – not the letter, but the sound). Language comprehension refers to the process by which words, sentences, and talk are interpreted. The two dimensions of reading can be represented in a grid, as seen in Figure 4.2, with word recognition and language comprehension along each axis. Children can be at any point within this grid with the following four possible key outcomes.

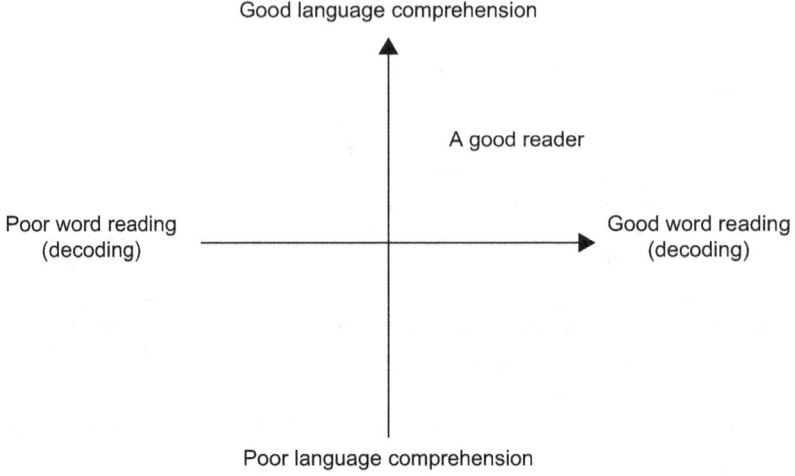

Figure 4.2 Simple View of Reading.

1. Learners may have good word recognition and good language comprehension
2. Learners may have good word recognition but poor language comprehension – meaning that they will struggle with the meaning of the text (often referred to as 'barking at print' and common in learners with ASD)
3. Learners may have poor word recognition but good language comprehension, which means that they cannot decode words to read any new text
4. Learners may have poor word recognition and poor language comprehension, which means that they cannot decode words to read any new text or the ability to understand

The model distinguishes between the processes required for each of these two dimensions. For example, the importance of teaching phonics is well acknowledged, alongside the repetition of tricky words in order to develop the word recognition dimension. When we think about the teaching of reading, we need to consider both of these dimensions as important and relevant to ensure that our learners have the opportunity to read with understanding, fluency, pace, and accuracy. The Reading Rope devised by Hollis Scarborough in 2001 and revised in 2010 provides a model that breaks down these two dimensions into key aspects.

The Reading Rope and learners with complex needs

Figure 4.3 provides an important illustration of the threads that are woven together to make each of the strands: language comprehension and word recognition. This is particularly useful within special education, whereby professionals have established practices that can be seen to fit within this model as approaches that will support learners to develop reading skills.

- For example, much of the curriculum content for learners with complex needs is focused around developing background knowledge, vocabulary, language structures, and literacy knowledge.
- It is useful to use the Reading Rope to discuss how activities such as the use of sensory stories contribute to learners' development of language comprehension skills, and to consider where they may be used to support word recognition for those where this may be relevant.

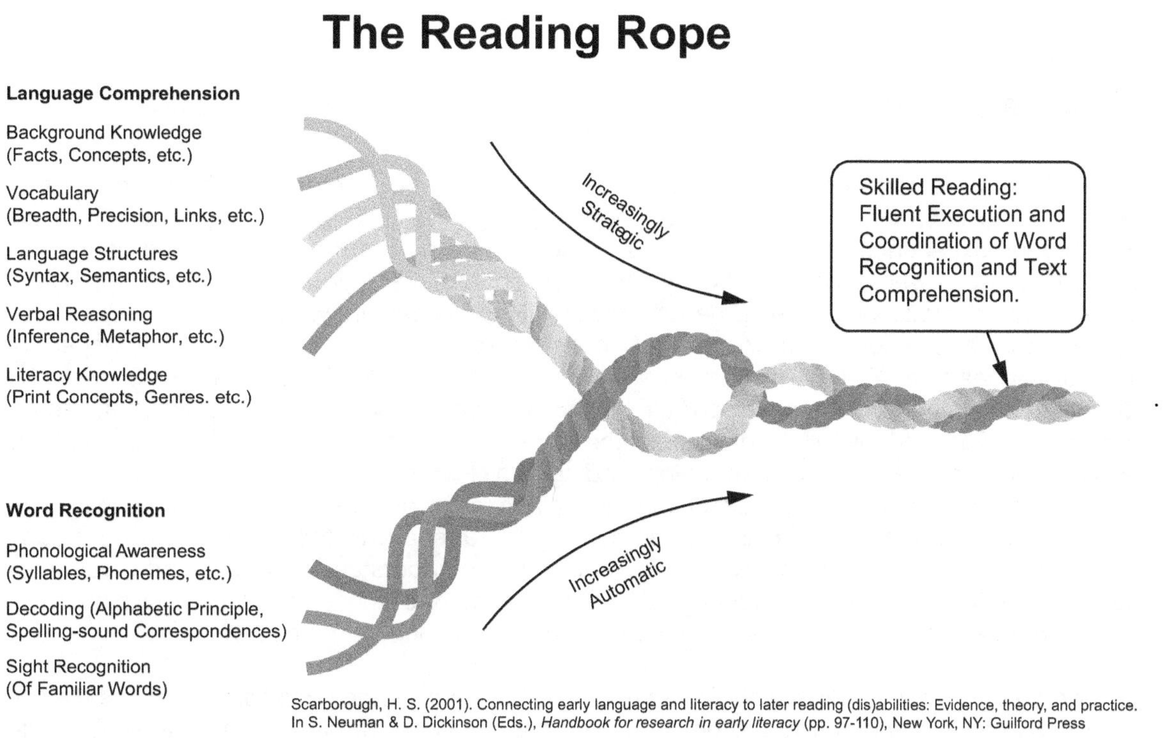

The Reading Rope

Language Comprehension

Background Knowledge (Facts, Concepts, etc.)

Vocabulary (Breadth, Precision, Links, etc.)

Language Structures (Syntax, Semantics, etc.)

Verbal Reasoning (Inference, Metaphor, etc.)

Literacy Knowledge (Print Concepts, Genres. etc.)

Increasingly Strategic

Skilled Reading: Fluent Execution and Coordination of Word Recognition and Text Comprehension.

Word Recognition

Phonological Awareness (Syllables, Phonemes, etc.)

Decoding (Alphabetic Principle, Spelling-sound Correspondences)

Sight Recognition (Of Familiar Words)

Increasingly Automatic

Scarborough, H. S. (2001). Connecting early language and literacy to later reading (dis)abilities: Evidence, theory, and practice. In S. Neuman & D. Dickinson (Eds.), *Handbook for research in early literacy* (pp. 97-110), New York, NY: Guilford Press

Figure 4.3 Scarborough's Reading Rope.

To become a skilled reader, learners need to develop both of these dimensions at the same time. The focus should be upon the development of language comprehension and word recognition across the week to ensure that each strand is formed securely.

As well as language comprehension and word recognition, learners must also be motivated to read. If learners are not supported to develop their understanding, enthusiasm, and appreciation for stories, poems, and narratives, they will not be motivated or engaged in the process of learning to read. Therefore, running alongside the two crucial skills demonstrated by the Reading Rope is the importance of engagement and motivation. It is through the development of all these aspects that we can support learners to read with fluency, accuracy, pace, and understanding. As summed up with the reading framework (DfE, 2021), "through enjoying rhymes, poems and songs, and reciting poems or parts of longer poems together as a class, teachers can build children's strong emotional connection to language".

How do they achieve this for learners with complex needs?

To become a reader, in the widest sense, it is important that the foundations for these skills are in place for all learners. This requires a focus on language and communication from the very beginning.

Learners with the most complex needs and disabilities may have

Fewer concepts about the world due to limited exposure to a rich literacy environment (*there are many reasons why this may be, but we are focusing on how to support learners*), alongside:

- Fewer opportunities to develop the prerequisite skills required that have to be taught, due to physical, biological, or cognitive needs
- Contexts whereby professionals have lacked access to relevant CPD, focusing on reading for learners with the most complex needs

We have the opportunity to support both of these issues!

Foundation skills

Influential research into prerequisite skills required for learning begins with the importance of being able to coordinate and control our bodies (Longhorn, 2001). This begins prebirth, and it is through experiences and opportunities to feel and be part of the world around us that we become aware of who we are and how we feel, and shared interactions begin to develop. Gaining literacy skills follows a developmental process; it is a continuum with no end.

This could be a whole book or series of books on its own, and it is an interesting aspect of including all learners. Early in my career, I was influenced by academics such as Les Staves who discussed the importance of developing 'Roots to Reading' (Staves, 2019). His diagram, seen in Figure 4.4, influenced me to look at some of the key aspects that can be considered foundational skills required for the pathway of teaching reading to all learners.

The foundations of literacy are developed as learners are provided with motivating and engaging opportunities to support their abilities to begin to attend and focus on the world around them. Crucial skills such as visual scanning, tracking, and understanding of the world around us support the development of later learning. The development of these foundation skills needs to be reframed as part of an inclusive reading curriculum. As Lacey emphasises,

> *for the most profoundly disabled learners, to be inclusive, literacy must also embrace the use of objects as a kind of text and perhaps even see someone learning to anticipate a favourite activity as learning to 'read' what is happening.*
>
> (Lacey, 2006)

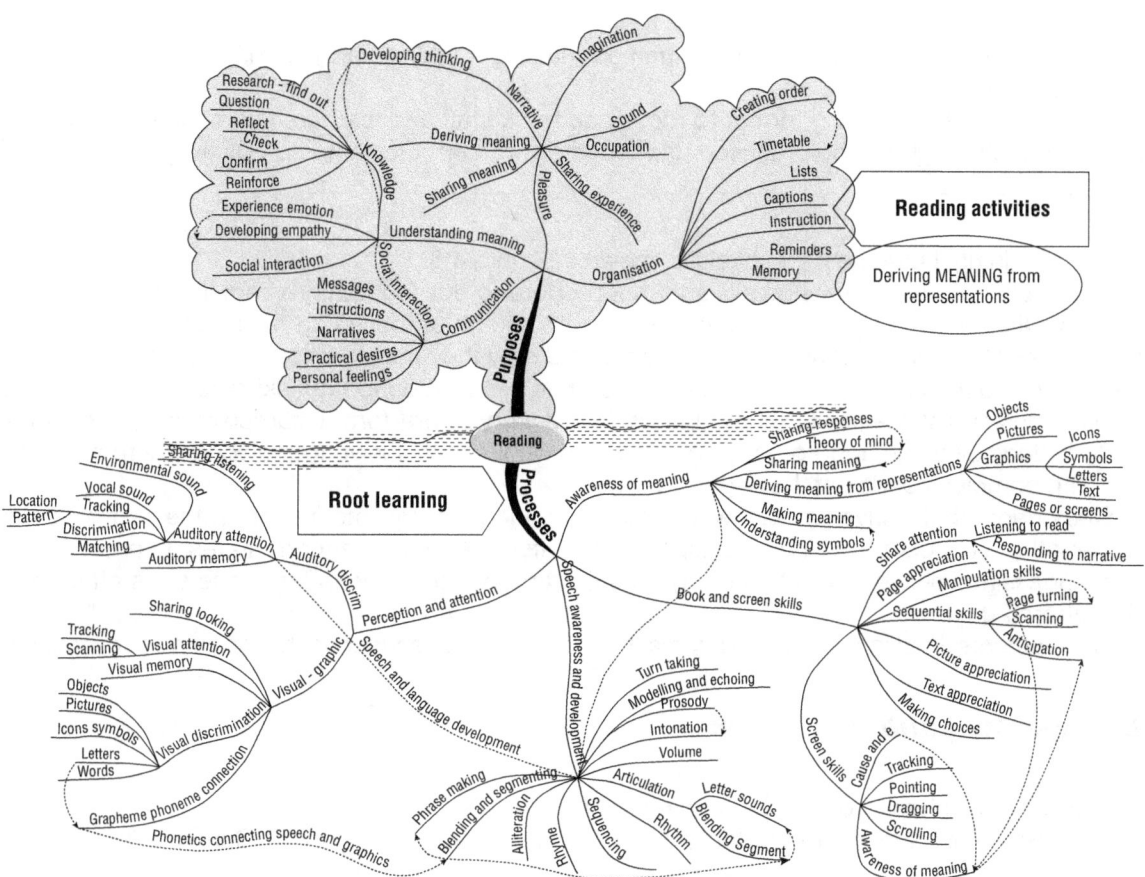

Figure 4.4 Roots to Reading by Les Staves.

Top tips for making the most of sensory stories with all learners

Written By Pete Wells

- For learners with profound and multiple learning difficulties, deliver in a rhythmic nature, with a steady hand clap, over several weeks.
- This rhythmic nature helps with consistent delivery and aids retention for the learner.
- The story is *always* delivered in the same location in my darkened classroom, with sound-reactive lighting.
- This is my strict routine, which acts as my sensory cue to let the learners know it is story time!
- Engaging sensory prompts are used to augment understanding, as well as to promote interaction, anticipation, exploration, communication, and engagement.
- Over time, you can clearly see progress in these areas as the learners begin to engage with the story.
- I make a multimedia version of the story using simple presentation software.
- This is linked to a switch to empower my pre-verbal learners to 'tell' the story, which is great for cause and effect, as well as for promoting that all-important self-esteem.
- The 'Story Massage Programme' (Mary Atkinson) converted it to a fantastic massage story. This enabled me to further deliver the story in an additional format, increasing awareness of the narrative and widening the context of the learning.
- For learners with less significant complex needs, engage sensory props and build sentences using colourful semantics (who-doing-what).
- Functional communication is key; practice expressive, receptive, and communication skills by answering targeted questions (e.g., 'quiz' questions using ChooseITMaker3).
- Use to support personal learning outcomes, e.g., communicating with or interacting with peers. Use multiple sets of props to encourage learners to explore props with their peers.
- Use as a vehicle for curriculum content, e.g., use switch-adapted technology to make ladybird biscuits, employing early mark-making skills to decorate various minibeasts,

> enjoying and interacting during themed massage, taking part in minibeast songs, and so much more.
> - Develop a motivating format to focus and hook staff and learners to enable somewhat repetitive skills to be practised and repeated with enthusiasm and positivity.

In my training, I use the cycle of skills shown in Figure 4.5.

The cycle consists of several skills that contribute to the foundations required for learning – and specifically, learning within literacy and reading. Each of these can be adapted to provide a framework of existing practice within schools, and how they are all linked together to provide an inclusive reading curriculum for all. I developed this cycle of foundation skills as a way to look at approaches and strategies used within existing sensory or pre-formal curriculums. This enables us to include all these good practice approaches within an inclusive framework, where all learners with complex needs can be seen as readers.

One school that I have worked with placed engagement and motivation at the centre of the cycle; other schools place it as an aspect within itself. As Flo Longhorn states, Literacy is the encompassing vehicle that offers many different approaches to learning these skills effectively (Longhorn 2001).

The elements that I include within my master diagram are described in the following subsections.

Engagement and motivation

- Engagement has to occur for learning to happen
- Engagement is the most important predictor of successful learning for all (Carpenter et al., 2015)

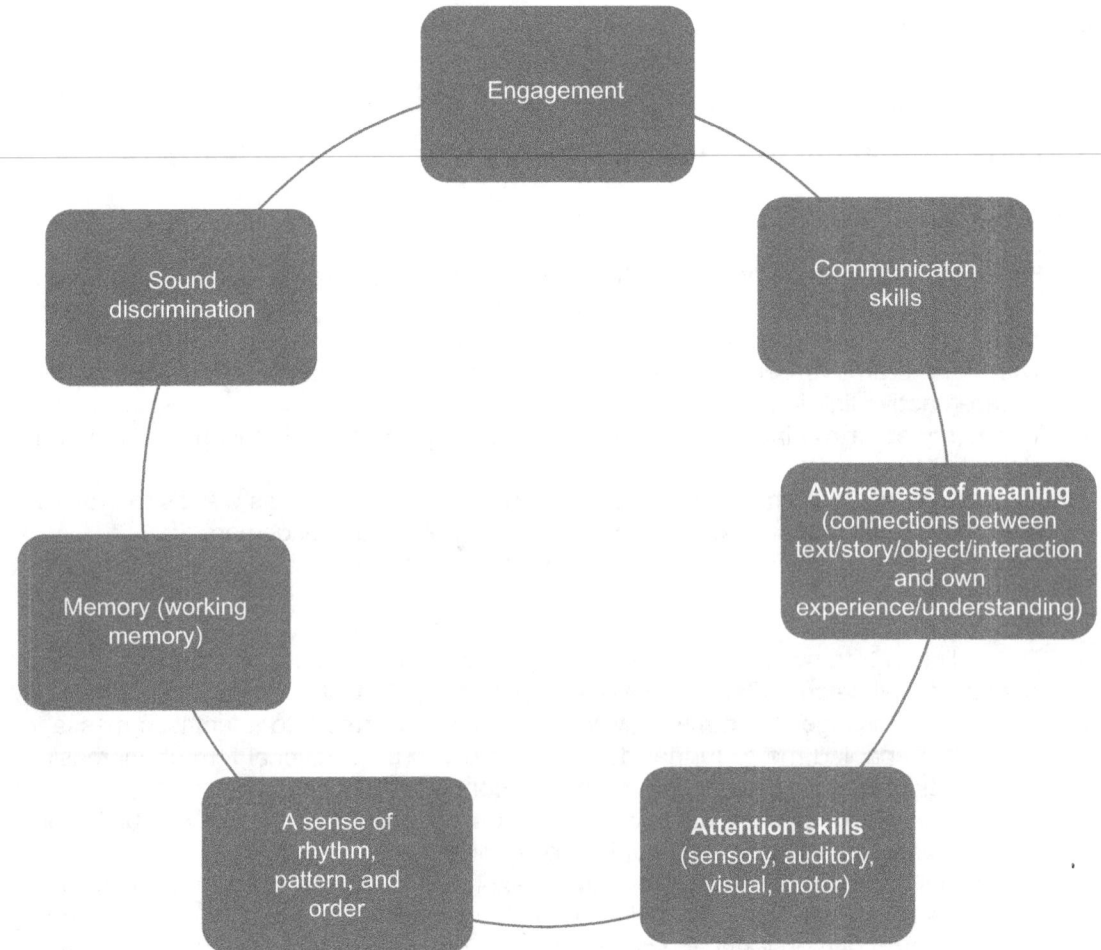

Figure 4.5 Foundation cycle of skills.

- The learner has to have the opportunity to encounter and the opportunity to be engaged
- Consider what engagement looks like for that learner
- Stress the importance of a strong belief that everyone can achieve learners and you can support them
- This requires enthusiasm and more enthusiasm

How to support this

- Connection between the learner and the environment is the key
- Keep it simple; use core elements that the learner displays awareness when encountering them
- Consider what aspects may lead a learner to switch off/reduce engagement (too much stimulus, or not enough stimulus)
- Provide opportunities for learners to explore the world outside of their immediate senses

Communication skills

- To communicate, we must be aware of others and want to interact
- Learners must be motivated to engage
- Literacy enables learners to use their creativity and imagination in a way that is different than any other forms of communication
- The development of communication is at the heart of all skills required for life
- Leading to an awareness of patterns, sounds, and meaning of symbols

How to support this

- Always have a personal communication system ready to go
- Activities that are based on a shared knowledge are central to this; literacy provides the perfect vehicle for this (shared stories, props, choice making, turn taking, shared attention, repetitive activities to build up a desire for more)
- Use core vocabulary that will support shared learning (indicate likes, dislikes, preferences, wants, and needs)
- Provide time to respond and wait with interest
- Respond to all communication offered; Project Core has some brilliant resources to support all aspects of communication with the motto "Every move is a chance to teach" (www.project.core.com)
- Create a communication-rich environment with meaningful activities in the natural context

Awareness of meaning

- Connections between story, object, interaction, text, and own experience understanding
- Provide access to learning, reducing barriers alongside motivating resources, activities, and literacy rich experiences
- Continued positive support, repetition, and a sense of fun
- Keep it consistent to enable a learner to make progress

Attention skills

- Development of attention starts with the senses
- From encountering to awareness and response
- Repetition enables this to be generalised and retained
- Supports understanding of the world and development of complex concepts

How to support this

- Access to stimuli using all senses (visual, auditory, touch, smell, taste, movement)
- Provide motivating stimuli to develop responses, movement, and concentration in relation to these

A sense of rhythm, pattern, and order

- Developing an understanding of rhythm, pattern and order; add the element of predictability to the world around us
- Being able to predict and understand our surroundings enables us to learn more effectively and feel more secure
- Regular opportunities to experience language-rich experiences such as poems, songs, and call and response enables a strong emotional connection to language to be developed (DfE reading framework)
- In turn, all of this supports the learning of new words and develops a connection between language and experience

How to support this

- Provide access to sensory cues and other ways to develop a sense of routine and predictability
- Provide repetitive opportunities to gain an understanding of established routines
- Provide lots of opportunities to experience rhythm, pattern, and order using music, language, sound, and sensory stimuli

Auditory awareness/sound discrimination

- The ability to attend and discriminate between sounds is a key foundation skill
- It is the foundation to later letter sound awareness, the ability to recognise the sounds words are made up of (phonics)
- The ability to attend to sounds – to listen, discriminate, and notice differences rather than just hear – is crucial to developing communication too

How to support this

- Music has the similar patterns of sound as speech and provides a fantastic vehicle for learning for all
- Use song/music as predictable starters to activities and daily routines leading onto providing choice
- Building up memory and recognition of sound, leading into discrimination
- Develop awareness of environmental sounds, familiar sounds and voices (understand they can make sounds), and respond to and recognise different sounds
- Exploring the sounds in words should occur as opportunities arise throughout the course of the day's activities, as well as in planned adult-led sessions
- Oral blending and segmenting the sounds in words; recognise alliteration (all important as pupils develop their ability to tune into speech sounds)
- As appropriate, connect letter to sound to grapheme-phoneme correspondence

Memory (working memory)

- Short-term/working memory can be a big hurdle for learners with complex needs
- Working memory helps to hold information that we need and discard information that is not important, manipulate objects, and pay attention
- This can be overloaded when learners need to focus on more than one thing, e.g., sitting on a chair, being overwhelmed with sensory information, or needing to physically manipulate a switch to access a activity
- Repetition leads to retention and enables generalisation and retention
- This supports understanding of the world and development of concepts

How to support this

- Provide predictable routines; reinforce and repeat what has been learnt
- Develop awareness of vocabulary and meaning of text through multi-sensory experiences

Seaside Walk
Written for the Story Massage Programme
www.storymassage.co.uk

	We go to the beach, crunching on the shingle.
	Seagulls swoop in and out of the waves.
	Sea sprays our faces, and we taste salt on our lips.
	A sudden shower drenches us, and we run for cover.
	Out comes the sunshine again, drying everything.
	Let's eat some chips on the beach, sprinkled with salt and vinegar.
	Look at the seagulls slyly eyeing up our chips.
	Listen to the happy sound of laughter as people play in the waves.
	The soft feeling of ice cream melting on our tongues ends our day in the warm sunshine.

Figure 4.6 Seaside Walk written for the Story Massage Programme.

- Provide concrete language-embedded experiences including listening, comprehension, vocabulary, and use of narrative (telling own stories)
- Use movement and sensory-based experiences to introduce/reinforce vocabulary and concepts

Time to think

What aspects of your current practice fit into the model of foundation practice?
Make a list of these and create your own cycle of foundation practice.

References

Adams, M.J. (1990) *Beginning to Read: Thinking and Learning about Print*. Cambridge, MA: MIT Press.
Carpenter, B., Egerton, J., Cockbill, B., Bloom, T., Fotheringham, J., Rawson, H. & Thistlethwaite, J. (2015) *Engaging Learners with Complex Learning Difficulties and Disabilities: A Resource Book for Teachers and Teaching Assistants*. London: Routledge.
Castles, A., Rastle, K. & Nation, K. (2018) Ending the reading wars: Reading acquisition from novice to expert. *Psychological Science in the Public Interest*, 19, (1), pp. 5–51 [online] Available at: https://journals.sagepub.com/doi/full/10.1177/1529100618772271 [Accessed: 30/06/2022]
Dehaene, S. (2009) *Reading in the Brain*. London: Penguin Random House.
Department for Education. (2020) Special educational needs in England: January 2020 Information from the school census on pupils with special educational needs (SEN) and SEN provision in schools.
Department for Education. (2021) *The reading framework: Teaching the foundations of literacy* [online] Available at: www.gov.uk/government/publications/the-reading-framework-teaching-the-foundations-of-literacy [Accessed: 23/06/2022]
Gough, P.B. & Tunmer, W.E. (1986) Decoding, reading, and reading disability. *Remedial and Special Education*, 7, (1), pp. 6–10 [online] Available at: https://journals.sagepub.com/doi/10.1177/074193258600700104 [Accessed: 25/06/2022]

Kuhl, P.K. (2011) Early language and literacy: Neuroscience implications for education. *Mind Brain Education*, 5, (3), pp. 128–142 [online] Available at: www.ncbi.nlm.nih.gov/pmc/articles/PMC3164118/ [Accessed: 03/05/2022]

Lacey, P. (2006) *Inclusive literacy* [online] Available at: https://studylib.net/doc/7569318/inclusive-literacy [Accessed: 23/05/2022]

Longhorn, F. (2001) Literacy for very special people [online] Available at: https://sites.google.com/view/flolonghornsensorybooksfreedow/home#h.j3m1v4enpi7s

Muter, V. (2003) *Early Reading Development and Dyslexia*. London, Philadelphia: Whurr.

Ofsted. (2019) *Education inspection framework* [online]. Department for Education. Available at: www.gov.uk/government/publications/education-inspection-framework [Accessed: 09/06/2022]

Scarborough, H.S. (2001) Connecting early language and literacy to later reading (dis)abilities: Evidence, theory, and practice. In S. Neuman & D. Dickinson (Eds.) *Handbook for Research in Early Literacy*, pp. 97–110. New York: Guildford Press.

Snowling, M. & Hume, C. (2006) Language skills, learning to read and reading intervention. *London Review of Education*, 4, (1), pp. 63–76 Available at: www.scienceopen.com/document_file/e2b57a2e-d408-4e00-8b38-ce1596047874/ScienceOpen/s6.pdf [Accessed: 18/06/2022]

Staves, L. (2019) Roots to reading illustration in person '*Very Special Literacy training*'.

Stuart, M. (2006) Learning to read: Developing processes for recognizing, understanding and pronouncing written words. *London Review of Education*, 4, (1), pp. 19–29 [online] Available at: https://discovery.ucl.ac.uk/id/eprint/1506983/1/Stuart_2006%20London%20Review%20of%20Education%20learning%20to%20read%20%202006.pdf [Accessed: 23/06/2022]

Such, C. (2021) *The Art and Science of Teaching Primary Reading*. London: SAGE Publications Ltd.

Sullivan, A. (2020) *Phonics for pupils with special educational needs* [online] Available at: https://s3-eu-west-1.amazonaws.com/s3-euw1-ap-pe-ws4-cws-documents.ri-prod/9781138353640/Phonics_for_Pupils_with_Complex_SEND_Companion_Booklet_2021.pdf [Accessed: 12/06/2022]

Wolf, M. (2017) *Proust and the Squid: The Story and Science of the Reading Brain*. London: Icon Books Ltd.

Zhao, T.C. & Kuhl, P.K. (2017) Effects of enriched auditory experience on infants' speech perception during the first year of life. In D.A. Olweus, F. Reimers, R. Holdsworth, A. Hargreaves & S.P. Heyneman (Eds.) *Prospectus*, pp. 1–13. London: Springer Verlag.

5 The role of foundation skills and the teaching of reading

Where does phonics fit for learners with complex needs?

The skills required to learn to read are built on the development of crucial foundation skills, as discussed in Chapter 4. In this chapter, the focus will be looking at the hotly debated topic of the teaching of phonics, and why we should integrate this into an inclusive framework for all learners. Among the questions asked by many professionals working within special education are the following.

- Why should we focus or change our approach to include phonics?
- How appropriate or useful is the teaching of phonics for learners with the most complex learning needs?
- How does a whole word approach fit into a phonics-based structure for learners with complex needs?
- "I did not learn using phonics, so why should we do this now?"

The aim of this chapter is to provide professionals with an understanding of why supporting all aspects of reading is important for those with significant complex learning needs.

My experience

I have always been puzzled by the process of learning to read. I do not have any memory of learning or understanding the relationship between sounds and letters; as I have said, I have issues with spelling and with reading or decoding unknown words. The more that I have read, the more that I am aware that I must have gained this understanding and this awareness somehow. The DfE reading framework (DfE, 2021) emphasises the teaching of phonics as being at the heart of reading. I know that my inability to sound out unfamiliar words and lack of confidence when reading aloud is because I do not have a confident grasp of grapheme-phoneme correspondence (GPC). That is the way that print relates to words and sounds.

The Simple View of Reading model (Gough & Tunmer, 1986) and the Reading Rope (Scarborough, 2001) place language comprehension and word recognition at the heart of becoming a good reader. The teaching of phonics is a process required for the decoding of words and has a core role to play within word recognition. It is not the only process, but it is important. Learners require a bank of words to be stored within the long-term memory to support fluent recall. This is where phonics is fundamental and why professionals should have an awareness and understanding of the important role it plays for all learners.

As with the teaching of reading, I advocate a wide definition of the teaching of phonics that is built on a continuum of the following foundation skills.

- An awareness of the difference between sounds around us (auditory/sound discrimination)
- An awareness different sounds in words (phonological awareness)
- An awareness of the smallest units of sounds in words (phonemes) and the ability to identify and play with individual sounds (phonemic awareness)
- An awareness of the concept that print relates to words and sounds

This knowledge is built through core literacy-rich experiences within an inclusive reading curriculum and develops through structured literacy teaching. Including an awareness of phonics and decoding within the curriculum for learners with significant complex needs does not mean that either:

- We are expecting all learners to become formal readers
- We think the use of a more formal structured approach to the teaching of phonics will ever be appropriate for some learners

It means that all learners are part of the reading journey. Learners are included within a framework of skills that support a greater understanding of the world around them. They are provided with opportunities to become readers in the widest sense. This is in the same way that a newborn baby is provided with rich emergent literacy experiences, rather than formal structured phonics. They have the opportunity to develop foundation skills to support wherever the journey may take them. This opens a more inclusive discussion about the teaching of reading and inclusion of all learners.

> ### Ideas in action: case study from a special school
>
> **School** – Jade Collinge, Long Churchill Park Academy.
>
> **Context** – Approximately 220 pupils from early years through to Year 14. Our learners all have varying special educational needs and will have a current statement of special needs or a current education health care plan (EHCP)
>
> **Intent** – To try an alternative method to support word recognition. Two pupils in Year 3 would not respond to any phonics-related activities. I have been teaching three pupils phonics since September, working on learning SATPIN and initial sounds. I have tried a variety of different materials and activities which include the letters and sound programme, multi-sensory approach, flash cars, tactile letters, songs, magnetic letters, and Bob Books, to name a few. There was no retention or interest in saying any sounds or recognising letters.
>
> **Implementation** – I started the 'Phonics for Special Needs' programme Book 1 and within the second session, all pupils could identify the sounds, continue the sequence of sounds, e.g., *spspsp*, independently and achieved various other activities. They had not previously been able to engage fully or focus on the tasks.
>
> **Impact** – The short, focused tasks seem to have really worked for them, and I have seen them apply the sound knowledge in other contexts. All of my classes are now on different books depending upon their individual level, and I have seen the same results with other groups on Book 3 last week, too.

Where to begin

During the last two years, there has been a shift in focus in the support I am offering to special schools. The request is for relevant and appropriate CPD to build knowledge around how reading develops and how this may look for learners with complex needs. This has been lacking for professionals within special education, and there has been a shift in expectations for learners with complex needs but no support to develop understanding and confidence of those expected to implement these changes. This needs to be built on an understanding of evidence-based research and the impact that this can have upon opportunities and outcomes for learners. The focus should be on what learners may require in addition to the curriculum they are already offered, as opposed to 'instead of' that curriculum.

We should be on asking the following questions.

- How can learners with complex needs be provided with opportunities to be part of an inclusive reading framework using the sensory and literacy curriculum?
- How can learners access a rich literacy curriculum, which provides them with text-based experiences to enrich the language opportunities that are around them?

- How can we use the Reading Rope as a basis for understanding the strands and threads all learners need the opportunity to experience?

The teaching of phonics would therefore be seen as part of – rather than instead of – a learner's reading curriculum framework.

So, what is phonics?

The renewed focus on the importance of explicit phonics teaching has shifted the current view within the UK education system from a balanced view to a more focused approach whereby structured systematic phonics (SSP) teaching is key (DfE, 2021). Phonics is teaching learners to read words using the relationship between sounds (phonemes) and their graphical representation of letters (graphemes). Phonics links sound you know, with graphemes you know, to access words within our long-term memory. Phonics is not the teaching of reading; it is one important part of the whole reading curriculum. There is strong evidence in research that the teaching of phonics is the most important foundation all readers need to develop (DfE, 2021). I would recommend following the reading ape on Twitter @TheReadingApe or reading their blog www.thereadingape.com; they sum up some of the research stating, "what emerges from the research is that phonological awareness is the strongest predictor of how easily a child will learn to read" (Reading Ape, 2021).

Phonics can be argued to 'jump start' progression towards fluent word recognition (Such, 2021). High-quality instruction and support are required to enable practice, which leads to fluency. Learners require the tools and strategies to be able to read; they need word recognition and language comprehension to work together to be able to comprehend and understand meaning. Learners with complex needs will often have a very different experience of language and literacy for many reasons.

Within mainstream education, the importance of the teaching of phonics has been established for many years. As young children develop, they will begin to make connections between language and print. They will begin to create a bank of sight words that have been built up over time. As they begin to understand the relationship between sounds and letters, they will move from recognising words by sight (this develops as they encounter words such as their name, McDonalds, Google or key shop signs) which have concrete visual representations, like pictures, to learning the difference between sounds that represent parts of words. They will need to become confident with the alphabet and the way that these letters combine to make 44 sounds!

The move from picture/words to phonics can be difficult for all learners. For learners with complex needs, this will be more problematic, but not impossible. They will require knowledge of the alphabet and awareness that blending sounds represented by letters is needed to read words. They will need the ability to remember verbal information, remember the sounds, and remember the order that they were in. Learners would also need a good verbal working memory in order to manipulate and move this information into their long-term memory. This is a complex task that requires a lot of brain energy and processing capacity. Research is clear that learners require repeated exposure over time to rich literacy experiences to support them to understand the alphabetic code founded on meaningful literacy experiences.

Phonological awareness

There has been a renewed understanding about the crucial role that phonological awareness (Figure 5.1) plays within the process of learning to read (DfE, 2021). Phonological awareness is a foundation skill for learning to read; it is the understanding of the way that language can be broken into smaller parts. This can develop from an awareness that spoken sounds have meaning to an understanding of words in a sentence; to the ability to recognise rhyme, syllables, onset, and rhyme; and to the ability to isolate beginning or end sounds. As this skill strengthens, learners may be able to segment and blend sounds or to add, delete, or change phonemes in order to read and write new words.

To develop an understanding of letters and sounds, learners need to develop an awareness about the sounds around them. They need to attach meaning to the context of these sounds and

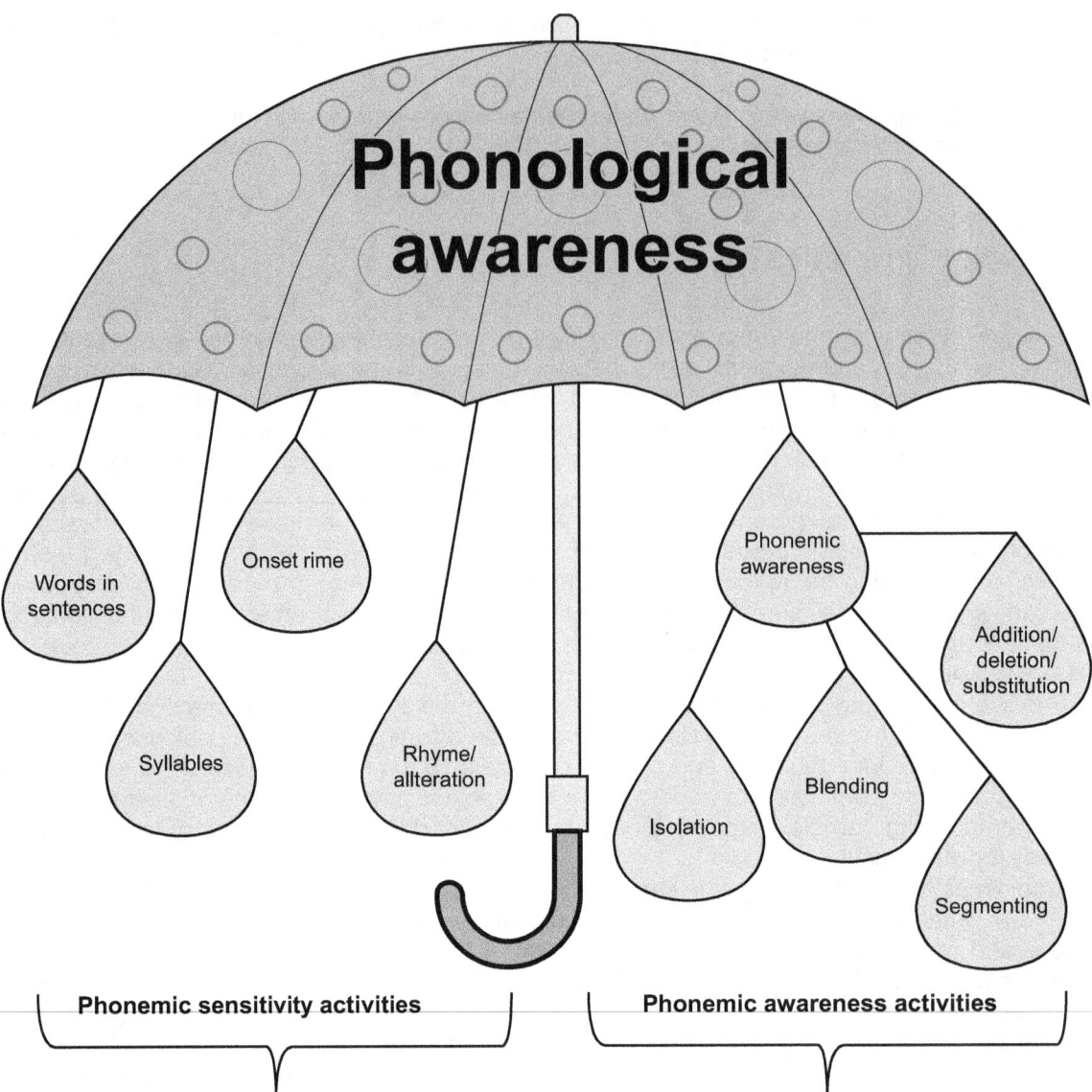

Figure 5.1 Phonological awareness poster by Phonic Books.

recognise that they are different. As discussed previously, this is called auditory discrimination and it is key to the development of language and reading. Auditory discrimination is the ability to notice the differences and similarities between sounds. This can be decoding the sounds from the environment, cars, animals, or units of speech; it is the foundation for phonological awareness to develop and for a learner to become a skilled reader. Skills development begins with experiences of sounds, language, speaking, and listening; the more, the better! For our learners with more complex needs, there will of course be issues in this area; we therefore need to initially consider communication and language in its widest sense.

Auditory discrimination

Auditory discrimination is one aspect of our ability to deal with sounds correctly, along with the following.

Figure-ground discrimination – The ability to filter sounds to attend to from background noise. The learner may have trouble following instructions and ask for them to be repeated.

Auditory memory – Remembering what we hear. The learner may have problems remembering nursery rhymes, unless written down.

Auditory sequencing – Remembering the order and sequence of sounds. The learner may mix up sounds of words.

Auditory processing disorder is when learners are weak in one or more of these aspects.

Learners with auditory processing issues find decoding and remembering what they hear difficult. They often miss – or misunderstand – information that is spoken in instruction or conversation. The ability to recognise differences between sounds is highly developed in a typically developing newborn. There has been an increase in the number of those entering school with deficits in auditory awareness or processing issues. For learners with complex needs, this will also be the picture, but they are further disadvantaged as this increase will be less easy to spot. There may be many reasons for an increase in the number of learners entering education with deficit language skills, including environmental changes, economic changes, changes in technology use, and changes in family structures. Babies who grow up in a noisy environment or where background or white noise dominates will have issues; they may learn to attend to the noise. If we consider the implications of this for learners with complex needs who may be surrounded by equipment noise or have sensory sensitivities, there may be a greater impact of this on skills.

The importance of sound

At the heart of an inclusive reading framework is an understanding of sounds around us. Active listening and noticing the difference or sequence of sounds is key to many later language skills. It is also important for our learners with the most significant complex skills. The ability to understand sound provides information about the world around them. Learners with visual impairment will gain most of their core information about what is happening around them by understanding the sounds they hear (Fraser, 2012). A greater understanding of sound and ability to tolerate these sounds will enhance learners' ability to be part of the world, aiding wellbeing and mental health (Aslan, 2021).

The ability to hear sounds, discriminate between them, and then begin to manipulate them requires an environment whereby learners are exposed to sound in an engaging and motivating way. Learners with complex needs can benefit from structured listening activities, whereby they are developing their understanding or awareness of sounds around them. Being taught about sounds, their meanings, and developing their tolerance to these, will have a positive impact on all learners. For example, learners with visual impairments gain information about the world around them through listening and interpreting sound. Therefore, sound can provide learners with an increased input of information about other people, relationships, the world around them, and their place within it.

In a pre-formal or semi-formal curriculum framework, there are many opportunities for learners to learn about and through sound. Music is often used to support learners with complex needs to engage with the curriculum and add motivation. Music has similar patterns of sound as speech with a predictable structure (a beginning, middle, and end) but can be far more motivating. Many schools will often use song or music as indicators that an activity is about to start or for key daily routines. By using music, learners can be supported to build up their memory and recognition of the differences between sound, leading to enhanced auditory discrimination. They can be provided with opportunities to listen and remember sounds (tune into sounds through music and rhymes together).

It is important that we recognise how creatively music is used currently within many pre-formal and semi-formal curriculums. At one end, learners are developing an awareness and tolerance of sound and beginning to develop the foundation skill of auditory discrimination; this will include the sounds within spoken language. At the other end they are identifying and manipulating sounds within words. For all aspects, learners need the experience and opportunities to be immersed in a rich literacy environment, to develop their knowledge about sounds and language that are all around them.

Ideas in action: Victoria from rhyming multisensory stories on the importance of sound

Sound effects breathe life into a multi-sensory story and provide the opportunity to elicit response from the story explorer. Consider the following.

Can the story explorer communicate our requests to listen to the sound again?
Can the story explorer track the sound?

> If using a prop or a single-switch communication device, can the centre explorer use/activate the prop device to make the sound?
>
> Can the story explorer imitate the sound?
>
> Can the story explorer record their voice and play it back?

Auditory discrimination and our reading framework

If we begin to look at the teaching of phonics as part of a continuum of opportunities and experiences that we already provide, we include all learners. As I have stressed throughout, the conversation should not be about either/or, but about a holistic view of the teaching of reading and the importance of including all learners within an inclusive reading framework. Providing aspirational learning opportunities for all should be at the heart of the framework.

Rich literacy environment

It is important that opportunities to develop auditory discrimination are within a rich and varied environment. We have discussed the importance of this in previous chapters and provided examples of ways that learners can be immersed in rich literacy experiences and environments. The focus should be on developing pupils' understanding of language and its meaning alongside its relationship to print. Daily speaking and listening activities that are well matched to pupils' developing abilities and interests – ones that use a wide definition of communication to include all learners – are important. There should be lots of listening activities related to text, including songs, stories, limericks, tongue twisters, alphabet songs, and rhymes. The importance is to ensure that these are engaging and motivating for learners of all ages and stages. We should begin with speech and move onto sounds within words including lots of opportunities for oral blending and segmenting the sounds in words. I have a great love of working with books, text, and resource is where alliteration is key.

> ### Ideas in action: case study from a special school
>
> **Context** – Alison Pettitt. Former special school teacher, parent of Timmy. I worked in a school for autistic children and had a KS1 class of pupils ranging roughly in ability from P2(i)–P4.
>
> **Intent** – One of my main targets for the class was to bring them together as a group several times a day and involve them in short, attention-grabbing, repetitive sessions which would give them positive, predictable experiences of the rhythm of language.
>
> **Implementation** – A story would run for a half term. My story was *Handa's Hen* by Eileen Browne. I broke it down into chapters, as it was too long for this class in its entirety, so the animals which were encountered in the book also became themes for other activities during the school day. As it was a short half-term, there were enough animals for two per week. So, for example, when it was 'mouse' week, we also looked for edible mouse sweets in jelly during our sensory play activity.
>
> I decided to write a simple chant to begin and end, as I had found that this sort of rhythm would hold the children's attention. I used a djembe to make the rhythm. This large instrument made a comforting African sound, not too loud for our sound-sensitive pupils but helpful to set the scene and maintain the children's attention.
>
> The middle section of the sessions would involve related objects to handle, taste, smell, or look at, along with a piece of music. So again using mouse week as an example, we passed round soft toy mice to handle, used a mouse on a stick (pet toy) to scuttle near the

> children, an electronic mouse zoomed around and we played the song – "a mouse lived in a windmill".
> I would then whisper – "could this be Handa's hen?", and the final chant went as follows:
>
> > Handa's hen, Handa's hen
> > We went looking for Handa's hen
> > Handa's hen, Handa's hen
> > We went looking for Handa's hen
> > We found _____, we found _____ [first animal]
> > We went looking and we found _____
> > We found _____, we found _____ [second animal]
> > We went looking and we found _____ .
>
> **Impact** – I found that those pupils who responded well to music also showed the same happy swaying and attention to the rhythmic chants. It was a joy to see them anticipating the beginning of the sessions when the djembe came out of the cupboard. This held their attention for considerable periods, and they showed clear enjoyment of the sounds.
>
> For one of our more able pupils who really struggled to sit still, we were surprised to see her bounce to the front of class and begin playing on the drum herself. She went on to choose to look at the *Handa's Hen* book, and make verbal sounds in the way of the chant. This would take place at other times of day, so it was always worth leaving the book out to see if she would pick it up and get engaged.

Exploring the sounds in words should occur as opportunities arise throughout the course of the day, as well as in planned activities. Kuhl (2011) demonstrated that babies are universal speech detectors; they have very well-developed auditory capacities. It is through the environment of hearing language or being exposed to rich language that the sounds of language are learnt and identified as meaningful. This is crucial to remember for learners with complex needs and could be an area in which we can reduce barriers and provide rich repetition of language in the environment.

Simply talking and creating opportunities for talk or for communication is key. For our learners with complex needs, we need to consider talking in the widest sense, as the exchange of information from one person to another in a meaningful context. As the learner experiences these communication exchanges within a meaningful context, the brain can connect and strengthen key neurological pathways. This creation of pathways is central to the development of possible later higher-order skills. If pathways/connections are not created, then the brain will have fewer processing skills available.

There needs to be consideration around the importance of linking the sensory-cognitive functions of reading – including phonological and phonemic awareness – in this. Multi-sensory teaching and learning opportunities are key throughout this framework, to ensure that activities continue to engage, motivate, and most importantly are accessible for learners with complex needs. As learners begin to develop phonemic awareness, they can be supported by creating mental imagery for sounds and letters within words. Most validated schemes have ways to support learners with this aspect using mental representations, such as dynamic imagery of actions, etc. At all stages of development, it is important to come back to this foundation development stage when introducing new and more complex sounds.

> **My experience**
>
> I have come full circle in terms of this debate, with a renewed understanding around the important role that whole word approaches can also play for learners with complex needs.
> Whole words refer to high-frequency words that learners need to know by sight to support them in progressing, engaging, and motivating the reading process. Whole word learning refers to words that can be instantly recalled from the memory regardless of how

it is phonetically made up. Whole word refers to a group or number of words that learners can recognise with very little effort. We see it and we read it. In many ways, we are still not sure about how children and young people learn to read. What we know is what areas are activated within the brain during the reading process, and therefore what we think may be happening. I recently read an interesting debate discussing outliers in research and the importance of not shutting off our minds to the wider understanding that what works for some may not work for everyone.

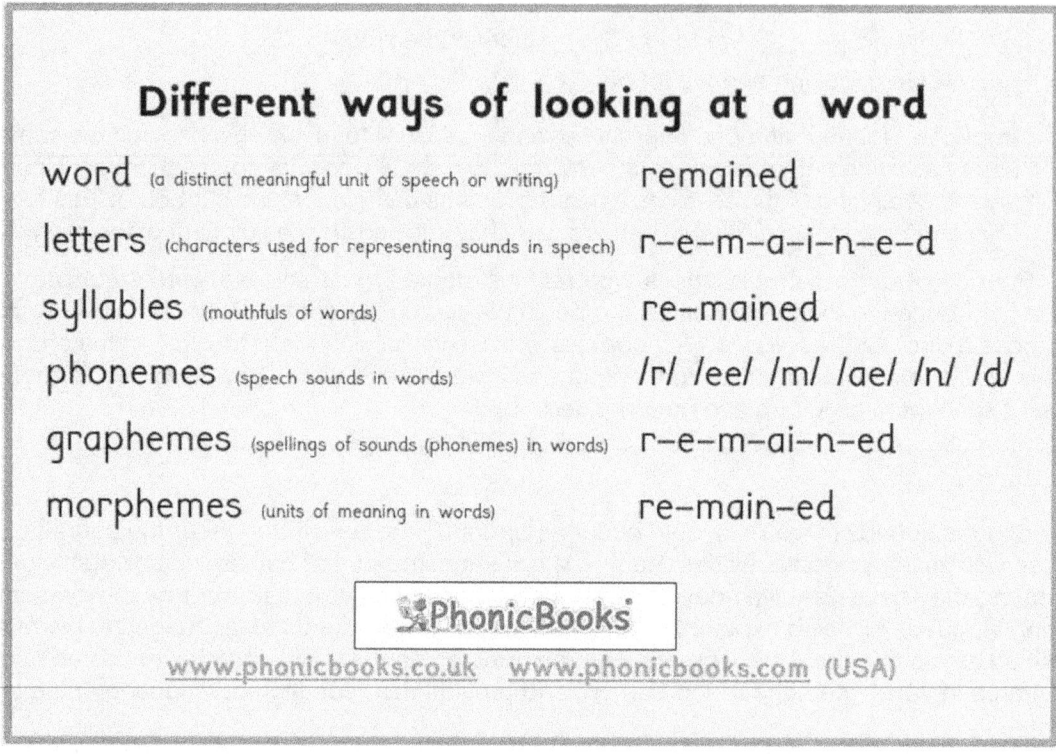

Figure 5.2 Different ways of looking at a word, by PhonicBooks.

The whole word vs. phonics debate

Once we have overcome the debate concerning the appropriateness or relevance of teaching phonics, the next question posed is: How does a whole-word teaching strategy fit in? As we have emphasised throughout this book, phonics is not a specific approach but rather the teaching of letters and sounds. There is no argument that reading is only about the teaching of phonics, although this has been interpreted as such by some. The argument here is that it may be more appropriate to use a whole-word method only for learners with complex needs. There are many reasons for this preference of approach, one being the research and the apparent success of such approaches. Being able to read a number of words, create sentences, make books, and label or name objects and pictures is something that is hugely motivating. In fact, being able to read a selection of letters or sounds does not in itself motivate or engage any learner.

It is important to define the difference between sight words, high-frequency words, and whole words as, often, these are used interchangeably.

Sight words

Words recognised instantly, dependent on times encountered and importance to the learner. They become sight words when there is no longer a need to decode them.

> **High-frequency words**
>
> Those that appear frequently in language that is written or spoken.
>
> **Whole-word learning**
>
> These can be either sight words or high-frequency words that are learnt using visual memory approaches, through repeated exposure to the written form of the word. This is often with an object, image, or audio to reinforce the meaning of the word.

Historically, research established that many learners with complex needs, in particular learners with Down's syndrome, can use a sight word or whole word approach to read and recognise many words (Bird & Buckley, 1994; Buckley et al., 2002; Buckley, 2007). This has led to several special schools teaching reading using approaches and strategies that have focused on a whole-word approach to learning with approaches such as 'see and learn.' More recently, reading develops in the same way for all. Instead we should consider that some require more support in key areas, such as more time on specific aspects, ensuring that there is motivation and engagement promoted during whichever method is used (Dehaene, 2009).

In fact, what is clear is that relying purely on memorising enough words without phonics could be seen as capping the learning opportunities of the learner. If we learn solely via our visual memory pathway, evidence has indicated that we can remember between 2,000 words and – for some – up to 5,000 words (Such, 2022). The English language requires the use of many more words than this. If we go back to the Reading Rope, we will see the ability to decode is an essential part of word recognition. If we look back at the Reading Rope and the evidence that has been discussed, decoding words and learning about this aspect is an important part of the teaching of reading.

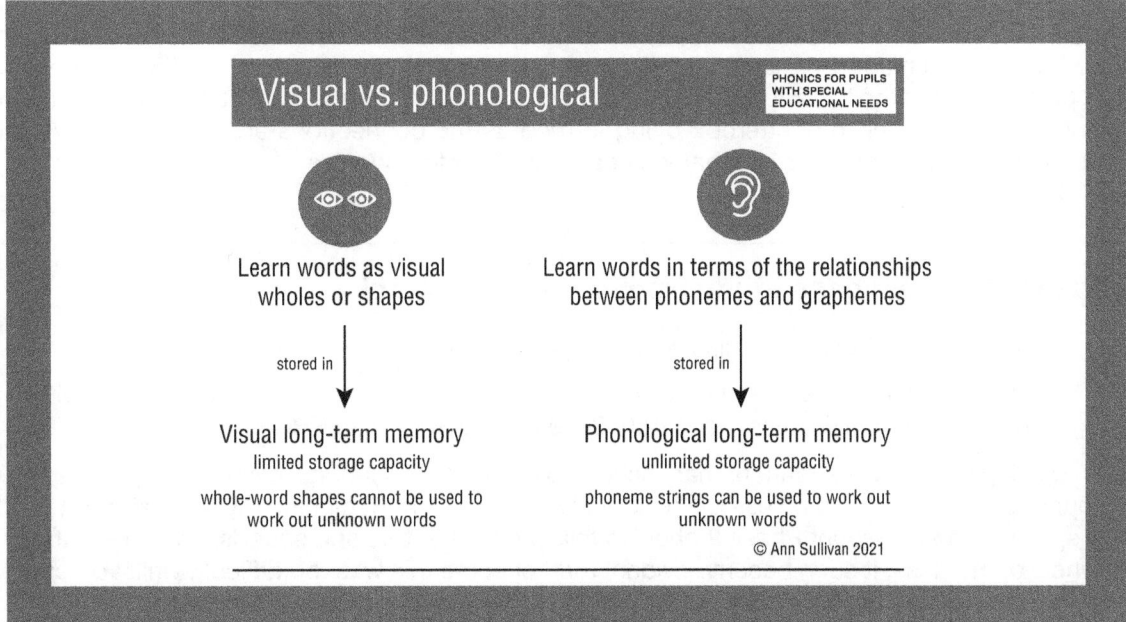

Figure 5.3 Visual vs. auditory pathways to learn to read, by Ann Sullivan.

The debate becomes further complicated by those who advocate that no word should be taught by sight or whole-word learning approach – that in fact all words should be taught through decoding approaches. By presenting polarised approaches or views, we are potentially reducing the chances of learners accessing the wide strategies needed to understand the English language. Recent evidence indicates a form of word poverty within education, that in fact all children and young people are lacking the vocabulary needed to flourish in the wider society (DfE, 2021). I would therefore suggest that we consider the following.

- Starting with methods that build confidence for all learners; this could be whole word or phonics-based reading approaches
- Provide rich literacy experiences to embed understanding in meaningful contexts
- Use the successes and confidence gained to develop all aspects of the reading process
- Build on and celebrate words known
- Build on and celebrate the sounds and letters known
- Monitor and review progress, adapting and supporting learners using a variety of strategies
- Move on to more formal approaches as appropriate

Orthographic mapping

It is important to be aware of the process of orthographic mapping and consider how our teaching supports learners' development of this. Grapheme-phoneme correspondence (GPC) refers to the ability to map the sounds of speech (phonemes) onto the letter representations (graphemes), and vice versa. Orthographic mapping integrates all aspects of the Reading Rope leading to sight word recognition. Cunningham et al. (2001) define orthographic processing or mapping as the ability to understand, store, and later access written representations of letters that are linked to sounds and the rules of the English language.

We apply this automatic alphabetic principle, and analyse every meaning of every word, engaging our executive functioning system (Ehri, 2014). Ehri emphasises that it is the connections that serve to 'glue' spelling to pronunciations in our memory, and we therefore connect what we see and hear, reading words instantly and activating both pronunciation and meaning (Ehri, 2014). Early reading is dependent on orthographic processing; this will not develop without phonological awareness. All learners need to experience language in meaningful contexts. For learners at any age or stage, hooking them into language and understanding of its relationship to text is fundamental to any development or understanding.

When we read aloud with a child, it leads to changes in the brain. As we hear the language read, neurons are activated, creating new circuits and stronger connections. Daily repeated exposure to rich literacy experiences is crucial to support learners to understand the alphabetic code. Aspects such as letter name identification, letter sound identification, identifying letters in text, and producing the letter forms are all key to this process (Jones et al., 2013). Research and scientific thinking refer to a letterbox being formed as the connections are made in the visual cortex area; research emphasises that we hear reading before we see it.

Ideas in action: case study from a special school

School – Melissa Holas Galley, North Ridge Community School, Doncaster.

Context – Northridge Community School is a special school catering for learners with severe learning difficulties, ages from 3–19 and each with an EHCP.

Moving from a mainstream primary school to a special educational setting, I have always taught phonics and reading using a 'whole-class' approach. Beginning my first half-term in a special school, I taught Phase 2 phonics following the letters and sounds structure to the whole of my class. It soon became evident that for some this was too difficult, whilst others thrived from the four-part structure and the systematic and sequential approach.

Intent – to develop the reading skills of all learners incorporating a clear structured phonics approach.

Implementation – All children accessed the same 'revisit, teach and practice' aspects. This ensured that all children were exposed to all of the Phase 2 sounds, regardless of their ability, and ensured that the children were not being 'pigeon holed', such that they could only achieve what I was allowing them to achieve. I then had three group settings.

What it looked like or involved: I taught a sound a day, on the following three-week cycle.

> Week 1 – Introduce a set of sounds, focusing on hearing, seeing, saying and the mnemonics for the sounds.
>
> Week 2 – Is a reading focus week, where children will look for the new sounds in words, read words, captions and sentences.
>
> Week 3 – Is a writing/spelling focus week, where children will learn to form the new letters and spell words with those sounds in them. This is where I would have previously used 'phoneme fingers' to spell, but due to the school being a Makaton school, this did not work for our children. Instead, I adapted this to using robot arms and chopping the word up into sounds that we could hear. I had adapted the 'apply' stage for each group so that the children were able to demonstrate their understanding and knowledge e.g. using magnetic letters for spelling.
>
> I taught the whole class and then we split off into three groups for the 'apply' stage. I would rotate the group I worked with to ensure that I knew how each of the children were progressing and to support my learning support teachers (LSA) with the delivery.
>
> **Impact** – By breaking the letters and sounds teaching structure up into a three-week teaching pattern, it took me a lot longer to deliver the whole of Phase 2. Once I got to the end, all the children had completed the Phase 2 phonic assessment. All groups demonstrated engagement and motivation throughout these sessions.

Print referencing

Things we can do:

- Page order: "We read this page first... Then we move to this page...."
- Point out the title of the book: "This is the title of the book. It tells us. . ."
- Point out text direction – top to bottom, left to right: "We begin by reading this word, and then we move..."
- Point to the text as you read – use your finger or a torch. Demonstrate how text goes from left to right, and then down a line. (Don't get the student to do this.)
- Talk about the author/ illustrator: "The author wrote this book – and they wrote the other book we read. . ."
- Talk about the front and back covers: "Here's where the book begins. It's called the front cover."
- Concepts of word: "Let's count the words on this page."
- Short/ Long words: "Which word is longer/ shorter. . ."
- Count syllables in words "This long word has three syllables, let's count them..."
- Point out words in illustrations / captions /subtitles: "Here it says 'mail' on the mailbox. . ."
- Talk about different types of punctuation and, where possible, why the author has used them e.g."it's a surprise and there's an exclamation mark"
- Talk about use of upper and lower case – make sure you use the label "capital letter" as well
- Talk about text items the author/illustrator uses to emphasise the content, mood, etc
- Talk about concepts of text order – first word, first letter, last word, last letter, first line, last line, etc.
- And more!!

Version 2, February 2021

Figure 5.4 Bringing text to life using print referencing, by Jane Farrall.
Source: https://www.janefarrall.com/wp-content/uploads/2022/01/Print-Referencing-2.0.pdf

The emphasis of the different approaches will shift as children progress; effective diagnosis can help to identify priorities and focus teaching to ensure that it is efficient. Oral language interventions which focus on spoken language and verbal interaction in the classroom appear to benefit all pupils (DfE, 2021). A focus on oral language skills will have benefits for both reading and writing. We need to start from a position whereby we consider that everybody can access the teaching of reading, for some more formal strategies and approaches may be inappropriate. For all, an awareness of the sounds that language is made up of should be part of this teaching.

> **My experience**
>
> During my research, classroom practice, training, supporting a wide number of special schools across the UK and my own parental journey of teaching a reluctant reader, I feel that certain views have dominated. We should not dismiss or ignore the importance of the teaching of phonics, but view it as part of the established good practice that exists across special schools and within the education of learners with complex needs. It is only through building on established good practice and integrating what is known to be effective in the teaching of reading for the majority of children and young people that we can truly move forward with an inclusive reading framework.

Never too late for phonics

Before we move on, it is important to consider the debate surrounding the applicability of phonics programmes for older learners. We have stressed throughout this book the important role that phonics plays within the process of learning to read. It is an important aspect for all learners, and as with other areas of teaching for learners with complex needs, the skills required may develop at a slower or in a different way. The foundation skills required – such as awareness of differences between sound, engagement with literacy activities, or an understanding of rhythm and pattern – will be developing at a different pace and stage. We therefore need to support and supplement this learning with continued awareness and understanding about the links between language, letters, and sounds.

In my experience, I have learnt a great deal about the importance of the teaching of phonics and using regular, repetitive, and systematic teaching alongside providing rich literacy environments and experiences. I am aware that in many schools, these aspects may not have been in place until the last few years. We need to ask ourselves after considering all this why we would think that learners reach an age when phonics may not be appropriate. What is appropriate is that we go back to the foundation skills required and ensure that the crucial roles of motivation and engagement are central to any inclusive reading curriculum provided. It is not about continuing to do the same thing, but rather looking at the barriers to learning, gaps, and skills that may be required and where the learner is heading. The focus should be on enrichment of literacy learning for all learners.

The next step is a greater understanding of the difficulties of barriers that some learners may face, specifically issues in stages of processing for learners with complex needs. An awareness of this will support us to have a better understanding of the strategies that will be the most effective.

> **Time for reflection**
>
> Considering your own experiences of learning to read, are you aware of what gaps that might be exist for you?
>
> Now considering some of the learners that you work with, make a list of the opportunities and experiences that you provide for them as part of their daily literacy curriculum. Are these supporting learners with the decoding and word recognition axis within the teaching of reading?

References

Aslan, M. (2021) Music therapy and PMLD. *SEND Magazine* [online], December 13 Available at: https://senmagazine.co.uk/content/specific-needs/pmld/15866/music-therapy-and-pmld/ [Accessed: 23/06/2022]

Bird, G. & Buckley, S.J. (1994) *Meeting the Educational Needs of Children with Down Syndrome: A Handbook for Teachers*. Portsmouth: University of Portsmouth.

Buckley, S. (2007) *Reading and Writing for Individuals with Down Syndrome*. DSE Enterprises [online] Available at: https://store.down-syndrome.org/products/reading-and-writing-for-individuals-with-down-syndrome-an-overview-pdf-ebook

Buckley, S., Bird, G., Sacks, B. & Archer, T. (2002) A comparison of mainstream and special education for teenagers with down syndrome: Implications for parents and teachers. *Down Syndrome News and Update*, 2, (2), pp. 46–54 [online] Available at: https://cdn.dseonline.app/pubs/a/updates-166.pdf [Accessed: 28/07/2022]

Cunningham, A.E., Perry, K.E. & Stanovich, K.E (2001) Converging evidence for the concept of orthographic processing. *Reading and Writing: An Interdisciplinary Journal*, 14, pp. 549–568 [online] Available at: https://link.springer.com/article/10.1023/A:1011100226798 [Accessed: 07/07/2022]

Dehaene, S. (2009). *Reading in the Brain*. London: Penguin Random House.

Department for Education. (2021) *The reading framework: Teaching the foundations of literacy* [online] Available at: www.gov.uk/government/publications/the-reading-framework-teaching-the-foundations-of-literacy [Accessed: 23/06/2022]

Ehri, L.C. (2014) Orthographic mapping in the acquisition of sight word reading, spelling memory, and vocabulary learning. *Scientific Studies of Reading*, 18, (1), pp. 5–21 [online] Available at: www.tandfonline.com/doi/abs/10.1080/10888438.2013.819356 [Accessed 14/07/2022]

Fraser, S. (2012) Transforming lives through music. *SEN Magazine* [online], September 12 Available at: https://senmagazine.co.uk/content/activities/1199/transforming-lives-of-children-with-sen-through-music/ [Accessed: 14/05/2022]

Gough, P.B. & Tunmer, W.E. (1986) Decoding, reading, and reading disability. *Remedial and Special Education*, 7, (1), pp. 6–10 [online] Available at: https://journals.sagepub.com/doi/10.1177/074193258600700104 [Accessed: 25/06/2022]

Jones, C.D., Clark, S.K. & Reutzel, D.R. (2013) Enhancing alphabet knowledge instruction: Research implications and practical strategies for early childhood educators. *Early Childhood Education Journal*, 41, pp. 81–89 [online] Available at: https://link.springer.com/article/10.1007/s10643-012-0534-9 [Accessed: 24/06/2022]

Kuhl, P.K. (2011) Early language and literacy: Neuroscience implications for education. *Mind Brain Education*, 5, (3), pp. 128–142 [online] Available at: www.ncbi.nlm.nih.gov/pmc/articles/PMC3164118/ [Accessed: 03/05/2022]

Reading Ape. (2021) What lies beneath – child development prior to reading [online] Available at: https://www.thereadingape.com/single-post/2020/08/18/what-lies-beneath-child-development-prior-to-reading

Scarborough, H.S. (2001) Connecting early language and literacy to later reading (dis)abilities: Evidence, theory, and practice. In S. Neuman & D. Dickinson (Eds.) *Handbook for Research in Early Literacy*, pp. 97–110. New York: Guildford Press.

Such, C. (2021) *The Art and Science of Teaching Primary Reading*. London: SAGE Publications Ltd.

6 Why learners have difficulty learning to read

Importance of the stages of processing and strategies to support

In this chapter, the processes involved in learning to read will be examined and the significant role that memory plays emphasised. Supportive approaches and strategies that can be used for all learners, including those with more complex needs, will be outlined. We will be looking briefly at brain development and unique differences that occur, and the existence of critical or sensitive periods for specific skills to develop alongside the impact of these on learners. The four stages involved in reading (input, integration, memory, and output) will be explained, and practical strategies suggested to support impairments or disabilities within these stages. The golden thread of engagement will be woven through all processes and the link with motivation explored. The chapter aims to provide a clear and workable overview of how we learn to read and relates approaches, strategies, and interventions, and how they may help reduce barriers to learning. The importance of accessibility and the use of technology will be touched on here, with practical ideas and strategies about how aspects of processing that may be barriers can be supported through these.

The four stages of processing required during reading

As emphasised earlier, children with learning disabilities are not a homogenous group. These children may approach the task of reading with uneven patterns of language skills, due to a variety of reasons, in comparison to typically developing children (Laing et al., 2001).

Dockrell and McShane (1993) discuss the importance of considering the child within a wider context. They point to three factors that need to be considered when trying to understand the learning disabilities a child may be experiencing.

1. The task – for example, how difficult it is
2. The child – for example, their cognitive ability or neurological damage that may exist (Rutter & Bailey, 1993)
3. The environment – for example, the teaching strategies used and the home background of the child

In this book, we are focusing on the importance of a structured approach to the teaching of reading, which relates to the environment and opportunities provided.

This is a useful approach for us to use when thinking about an inclusive reading framework.

- If we consider the task or activity, we need to look at how accessible this is for our learners and how engaging or motivating it is; we need to consider the age and stage of our learners
- If we consider the individual learner, we have to be aware of the influence that a neurological impairment, sensory deficit, or physical disability may have which influences the outcome

The brain develops with the same basic structure for everyone, but there are a number of possible ways that individuals can further develop, causing unique differences between people (Goswami, 2004). Although development of the brain is emphasised to be continuous, research has suggested the existence of critical or sensitive periods for specific skills to develop (Goswami, 1994). If these periods are missed, it may be that certain skills are not able to develop to their full potential (Goswami, 2004).

The complexity of the brain structure means that any neurological damage can result in a mixture of problems (i.e. sensory impairments, attention deficits, fine or gross motor control, poor short-term memory) affecting cognitive and linguistic skills in different ways (NICHCY, 1997). A model of learning disabilities presented by the National Dissemination Centre for Children with

Disabilities (NICHCY, 1997) distinguishes four stages of processing required during the learning process. The stages can be described as the following.

> Input – Where information is recorded from the senses
>
> Integration – Where this information is interpreted and organised
>
> Memory – Where the information is stored: sensory memory, short-term/working memory, and long-term memory
>
> Output – Where the information is accessed and used (e.g., speech)

Reading problems can be rooted in any of these four stages. Reading requires familiarity with the language system and awareness of the relationship between letters and sounds; therefore, learners with hearing impairments will have problems at the input level. The output stage requires muscular ability to produce the information through speech. In between these are the ability to interpret information from our senses and use our working memory to access information from our short-term and long-term memory. Learners with SEND may have deficits in any of these areas. This will result in complex learning patterns and needs.

There has been a re-emergence of a greater understanding of psychology – specifically, memory – as crucial to teaching and learning for all learners. In particular, learners with AAC and complex needs have specific issues relating to memory. Figure 6.1 provides a simplified view of the processes involved in remembering. It is through rehearsal and repetition that information is transferred to our long-term memory. Both auditory and visual coding of information (the way information is changed and stored) is the key to information being remembered. As pointed out earlier, this is where issues can exist for our learners with more complex needs, and it is important to understand this.

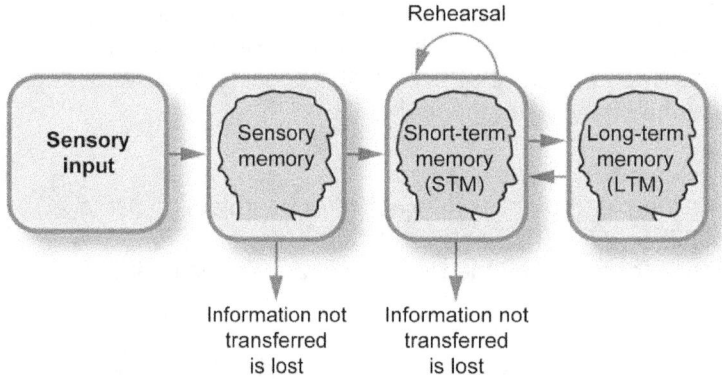

Figure 6.1 Atkinson-Shiffrin model of memory.

Licensed under CC BY 4.0

The role of us as professionals is to find ways to remove or reduce these barriers to learning and support all learners. Those with the most complex needs often have massive spikes in skills, abilities, and areas where deficits may exist. We may never know exactly what the issues are, but we can try to use good practice approaches and scaffolding to support learners to reach their full literacy potential. Finding out what processing issues may be preventing access to learning enables us to personalise activities and provide opportunities to develop and support where needed.

Input

This is where information is recorded from the senses, e.g., seeing words, pictures, and people; hearing sounds, music, voices; and perceiving touch and movement. A multi-sensory approach will support all learners at this input stage, and strategies that promote learning in this way are used across the curriculum and specifically in the teaching of phonics. Activities based purely on language or abstract ideas will be difficult for many learners, and specifically those with complex needs, but the addition of meaningful sensory experiences, pictures, and active manipulation of objects provides an accessible way in for all. This again brings us back to the importance of all learners being actively submerged in a literacy-rich environment, with multi-sensory approaches to enable information to be inputted and integrated. Activities should ensure a repeated exposure to language and text making the most of sensory resources and ICT to bring stories to life and bring information to all of the learners' senses (immersive sensory experiences – spaces, environments). At the input stage, the focus should be on providing meaning for learners.

Integration

Integration refers to the process whereby the information that has been received is stored so that learners can use it again. In my training, I discussed this as similar to putting away the shopping once we get home, making sure that items are in places where they can be found and used by others. The important factor at this stage is that information is seen to be meaningful and placed with other similar information. This requires learners to be attentive and engaged with the learning opportunity.

Memory

This is where the information is stored: sensory memory, short-term/working memory, and long-term memory. Memory can be conscious and unconscious; for example, explicit memory is conscious and something people can talk about. This aspect is where we believe that what we remember is what happened, but in fact, we are only aware of our explicit memory. Our implicit memory is what we know that is learnt through our life experiences and becomes so ingrained that it becomes a natural response. Unfortunately, this can lead to unconscious bias about our memories and thoughts that relate to what we expect, past experiences, or persuasion later on. This is the aspect that causes problems and is why our perception during the encoding stage is key.

Working memory

Working memory is the term used by psychologists to refer to the process that enables us to hold and manipulate information in our minds (Gathercole & Alloway, 2008). In the current educational climate, working memory receives a great deal of attention, and the focus is on looking at strategies to support learners to maximise this mental workspace, as it is crucial for all areas of learning. There are huge variations in ability, in terms of capacity, within us all – and this is key when we consider learners with complex needs. It may be that those with the most profound and multiple needs have little or no working memory capacity (Imray, 2021).

Working memory and cognitive overload have been highlighted as key areas where problems can occur for beginning readers. Reading requires familiarity with the language system and awareness of the relationship between letters and sounds; children with hearing impairments will have problems at the input level. Learners with complex needs will have issues here due to a reduced or restricted working memory. They will struggle as their working memory becomes overloaded easily, leading to problems transferring information to the long-term memory, giving problems at the memory stage.

It can be viewed as a box that can only contain so much information, and when we try to do too many things at the same time (focus on a new word, try to decode this word, listen to instruction, or sit still on our chair and hold a book or device), it overflows. There is a strong link between working memory and a learner's ability to focus and learn. It is through rehearsal and repetition that information is transferred to our long-term memory. Both auditory and visual coding of information (the way information is changed and stored) is the key to information being remembered. There are many strategies and interventions aimed at supporting a learner's working memory. Awareness of the issues that learners with complex needs may face in this area should inform the strategies and approaches used.

- Encoding of information is supported by context; therefore, information that is linked to a story or situation is encoded and remembered more than information that is stand-alone.

- In the same way, information can be retrieved and created to fit a context or story to support it making sense to a person.
- As learners progress to reading within a semi-formal curriculum, demands on working memory increase.
- Learners need to use prior knowledge to remember and to understand meaning between text and language/objects.
- Prior knowledge enables us to comprehend new material and new topics.
- Prior knowledge enables us to manipulate and work with letters and sounds, and it is therefore fundamental to later learning to read processes.

To support our memory and enhance learning, there are strategies that we can use which focus on changing the environment or providing learners with strategies. These can include the following.

- Structuring the environment to make it predicate
- Providing cues to routines
- Making connections between information; for example, using personalised stories, prompt cards, or mind maps
- Relating information to prior learning, reminding students where information is linked (use visual reminders and props)
- Overlearning and the use of repetition and revision; these are crucial for information to be transferred to long-term memory
- Presenting information in small amounts on a regular basis
- Focusing on repeating rather than testing; learners should view this strategy as a way of supporting them, not as a way of assessing what they have learnt
- Teaching pupils to 'chunk' information into smaller bits, e.g., to support remembering a long list of words, create groups of similar words (animals, foods)
- Creating multi-sensory activities to engage more than one sense, providing multiple routes for the information to reach the brain
- Reducing anxiety for learners, as anxiety and stress take up large amounts of space within our brains and can limit the capacity to take in new information; by reducing a learner's anxiety and minimising their feelings of difference, we are able to create more space for new information
- Promoting positive emotions and feelings to support motivation and engagement
- Scaffolding learning, gradually moving to longer periods of independence

---

Output

This refers to the information that comes from the learner in the form of speech, signs, gestures, or other communicative methods. There are many strategies to support output for learners which include signing, AAC, symbols, text to speech, or speech to text. All learners should have a way of communicating and interacting with those around them, and the development of this is one of the foundations required for an inclusive reading framework. If we provide learners with the ability to manipulate language and text, we enable greater flexibility in terms of what they would like to communicate and richer opportunities to communicate with others.

It is at the output stage that technology is key, as it provides not just accessibility but also motivation and engagement through increased visual and auditory information. Technology can be used to tap into learners' motivation or aspects the learner is really interested in, and it can provide immersive environments for all learners.

The use of symbols

Before we move on, it is important to mention the role of symbols within the teaching of reading. Symbols are a more abstract form of pictures and are used widely in special schools to support communication and the teaching of traditional orthography. Lacey (2006) found that 96% of the schools visited used symbols in some form, but most frequently, they were used within picture communication systems. Symbols can be used to support and enhance the meaning of text, as they provide the reader with increased visual information (Carpenter & Detheridge, 1994). Symbols can help to increase learners' ability to access literacy activities in a meaningful way, increasing autonomy, which in turn may have a positive impact on their social, emotional, and personal development. In terms of using symbols as an aid to the teaching of reading, rather than purely as a way into communication, some research has found that they may not be overly useful (Sheehy, 2001).

It has been argued that the additional cues provided by the image may cause a blocking effect to the learning of single words and more complex text (Ehri & Wilce, 1982). For many learners, the learning of symbols does not transfer to later word recognition, with systematic teaching required for them to be used effectively (Abbott & Lucey, 2005). Evidence suggests that pairing symbols with text makes the task of reading more difficult, and a decision must therefore be made as to why you would be using symbols when they can add to confusion and cognitive load. In my research, I used whole words on one side of a card and symbols on the other side. This was found to have very successful results with most of the participants.

Ideas in action: case study from a special school

Context – Ceanna MacGregor, principal teacher, Greenburn School, East Kilbride. Greenburn is a special school for a wide range of learners with complex needs ages 4–12. I have always valued reading activities as a fantastic way to develop

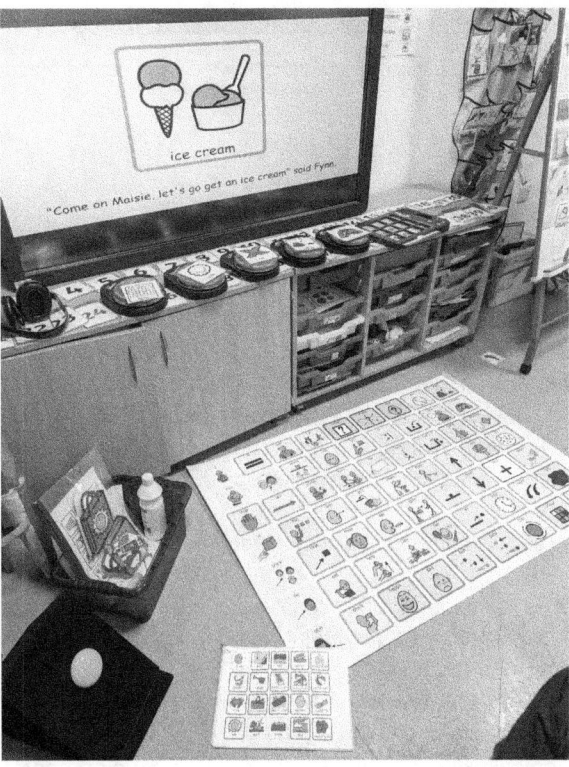

Figure 6.2 Using props, photos, ACC, and text to participate in shared reading of the story. Ceanna @communi_con provides lots of examples of ways that symbols and AAC can support learners communication, leading to accessible literacy opportunities.

> communication and literacy skills. After completing some training modules sponsored by Teach Us Too, I realised that I could be doing more to create a literacy-rich environment for the students I work with.
>
> **Intent** – I began to include more text and alphabet work in my teaching.
>
> **Implementation** – I supported sensory stories with printed versions of the stories. I began to target more letters and words in activities related to the stories. I also added visuals that include the whole alphabet, something I was guilty of not doing enough of before but will continue to improve on. Alternative pencils and predictable chart writing are now becoming favourites in lessons, too. I also created books for classes of things we had done – e.g., going for walks – and included photos and simple text.
>
> **Impact** – I have been delighted with the results! Many students who previously had not been highly engaged during stories have participated in different ways; for example, some paid more attention to the images we were discussing and comments being made. Some children who had not appeared to acknowledge letters were now seeming aware of or interested in the print, as well as the images. With writing, learners engaged in many ways, including choosing photos and pictures and choosing letters – whether at random or with intention. I am confident that improvements have been made in many areas.

In Chapter 7, I will bring together the information presented throughout this book and look at practical ways of creating an inclusive reading curriculum.

> **Time to think**
>
> Considering your own practice, how do you support learners with input, integration, memory, or output?
> Do you have any other ways that might be successful for your learners?

References

Abbott, C. & Lucey, H. (2005) Symbol communication in special schools in England: The current position and some key issues. *British Journal of Special Education*, 32, (4), pp. 196–201 [online] Available at: https://nasenjournals.onlinelibrary.wiley.com/doi/10.1111/j.1467-8578.2005.00397.x [Accessed: 23/05/2022]

Atkinson, R.C. & Shiffrin, R.M. (1968) Human memory: A proposed system and its control processes. *Psychology of Learning and Motivation*, 2, pp. 89–195 [online] Available at: www.sciencedirect.com/science/article/abs/pii/S0079742108604223 [Accessed: 25/05/2022]

Carpenter, B. & Detheridge, T. (1994) Writing with symbols. *Support for Learning*, 9, (1), pp. 27–32 [online] Available at: https://nasenjournals.onlinelibrary.wiley.com/doi/abs/10.1111/j.1467-9604.1994.tb00152.x [Accessed: 18/06/2022]

Dockrell, J. & McShane, J. (1993) *Children's Learning Difficulties: A Cognitive Approach*. Oxford, UK, Cambridge, USA: Blackwell.

Ehri, L. & Wilce, L. (1982) The salience of silent learners in children's memory for word spellings. *Memory and Cognition*, 10, (2), pp. 155–166 [online] Available at: https://link.springer.com/article/10.3758/BF03209217 [Accessed: 02/06/2022]

Gathercole, S. & Alloway, T. P. (2008) *Working Memory and Learning: A Practical Guide for Teachers*. London: Paul Chapman Publishing.

Goswami, U. (1994) Phonological skills, analogies, and reading development. *Reading*, 28, (2), pp. 32–37 [online] Available at: https://onlinelibrary.wiley.com/doi/abs/10.1111/j.1467-9345.1994.tb00834.x [Accessed: 09/07/2022]

Goswami, U. (2004) Neuroscience, education and special education. *British Journal of Special Education*, 31, (4), pp. 175–183 [online] Available at: https://nasenjournals.onlinelibrary.wiley.com/doi/abs/10.1111/j.0952-3383.2004.00352.x [Accessed: 24/06/2022]

Imray, P. (2021) A different view of literacy. *Support for Learning*, 36, (2) [online] Available at: www.researchgate.net/publication/350756737_A_different_view_of_literacy [Accessed: 27/06/2022]

Lacey, P. (2006) *Inclusive literacy* [online] Available at: https://studylib.net/doc/7569318/inclusive-literacy [Accessed: 24/07/2022]

Laing, E., Hulme, C., Grant, J. & Karmiloff-Smith, A. (2001) Learning to read in Williams syndrome: Looking beneath the surface of atypical reading development. *Journal of Child Psychology and Psychiatry*, 42, (6), pp. 729–739 [online] Available at: https://pubmed.ncbi.nlm.nih.gov/11583245/ [Accessed: 02/07/2022]

NICHCY. (1997) *Interventions for Students with Learning Disabilities*. Washington, DC: National Information Center for children and Youth with Disabilities.

Rutter, M. & Bailey, A. (1993) Thinking and relationships: Mind and brain (some reflections on theory of mind and autism). In S. Baron-Cohen, H. Tager-Flusberg & D. J. Cohen (Eds.) *Understanding Other Minds: Perspectives from Autism*. Oxford: Oxford University Press.

Sheehy, K. (2001) Teaching non-readers with severe learning difficulties to recognise words: The effective use of symbols in a new technique. *Westminster Studies in Education*, 24, (1), pp. 61–71 [online] Available at: www.tandfonline.com/doi/abs/10.1080/0140672010240106 [Accessed: 23/07/2022]

7 Practical ways into planning for an inclusive reading curriculum

This chapter focuses on creating an inclusive reading curriculum for all learners, developing word recognition and language comprehension across all curriculum pathways. The importance of motivation and engagement is the golden thread that runs throughout the framework. There is a focus on the importance of using a multi-sensory approach, alongside the inclusion of developing an understanding and confidence in the teaching of phonics. The teaching of language comprehension is discussed in the context of ensuring we provide all learners with a rich literacy environment, with a wealth of opportunities to access text, stories, and reading in many ways. The use of technology to enhance and ensure access for all learners will be discussed.

Where to begin

When I support schools with the developing an inclusive reading framework, I always begin with the following questions.

- Where are you now?
- What do you currently have in place to support learners across the pre-formal, semi-formal, and formal curriculum pathways?
- Where would you like to be?

This comes back to the learner being at the heart of everything that should be in place. As I have discussed throughout this book, this starts with each of us and our role as a professional. What expectations do we have about the role of literacy, and specifically the teaching of reading for the education of all learners? Is this reflected in the environment that we provide for all learners across all areas of the school? If we consider Figure 2.2 that I introduced at the start of this book and look at the building blocks that are required for all learners, we are able to begin to unpick where we would like to be.

Figure 7.1 Foundations of reading development.

It is important that we consider not only our expectations, but the expectations and ethos of our school and wider community of families and multidisciplinary professionals. Is there an understanding about the importance of teaching reading to all learners? This goes back to the role of establishing a shared vision and approach. This needs to be based on a shared

DOI: 10.4324/9781003220046-8

understanding about why the teaching of reading should be part of the curriculum framework for all learners.

> **Questions to ask and points to note**
>
> - Do all learners have the opportunity to be part of a rich literacy environment?
> - What activities, strategies, and approaches are already in place for learners across all curriculum pathways?
> - List ways that learners are supported across all pathways within the school. For example, if we focus on communication skills, look at how they support learners to show a preference, to make a choice, to indicate yes or no, or to functionally use AAC.
> - How do you develop and support learners with a preferred communication method, and how is core vocabulary developed and incorporated across the curriculum?
> - If we are looking at the sense of rhythm, pattern, and order, how do you provide access to sensory cues for all learners? Supporting them to respond and recognise these and gain an understanding of established routines and individual timetables?
> - Ensure we continue to provide all the regular and rich opportunities to experience the rhythms in music and language as well as sensory stories, songs, poems, limericks and more.

Developing a shared understanding

To develop a shared understanding, we must ensure that there is a structure of support and development in place. A review of current provision in terms of the teaching of reading and the needs of learners – including assessment, monitoring, allocation within current timetables, and strengths of staff – is required. Some of the key priorities for this could include the following.

- Ensuring that there is a shared vision that is reflected across everything that we do and that is reflected across all paperwork and structures (school improvement plans, website, policies, timetables, staff meeting agendas, training programmes, etc.)
- Providing training on intention and implementation of any change
- Looking at expectations for all pupils, monitoring, provision, and impact (gathering evidence to demonstrate and share good practice)
- Providing continued support for all members of our community to understand the impact of any changes that may be happening
- Providing continued professional development around the teaching of reading, including up-to-date training on research in this area and its relevance to the learners
- Providing opportunities to see practice being modelled and the impact this demonstrates for all learners
- Providing regular opportunities to share examples of good practice and ideas
- Ensuring that expectations around the importance of a rich literacy environment are demonstrated across the school
- Making clear expectations around financial decisions and budget allocations. Taking on board the importance of providing and updating literacy environments that are engaging and accessible for all
- Providing opportunities to be involved in coaching practices, to support and develop this shared understanding
- Ensuring that information is shared regularly via website, home–school communication, training, and workshops for the wider community, and more

> **Ideas in action: extract from St Francis special school reading policy**
>
> ### Pre-formal reading
>
> *Reading and storytelling should form part of ALL pupils' experiences. This may be through drama, real books or sensory stories.*
>
> At St Francis, we believe that reading and storytelling is important for all our learners. Not only do the pupils gain enjoyment from it, but it provides important skills and

opportunities for independence. Literacy and language is all around us. Children who are read to regularly have a much broader vocabulary. We need to provide our pupils with that enrichment. Our pupils have many different learning profiles, and therefore, each reading programme structure is linked to the individual pupil's need. Learning the alphabetic code is crucial in order for pupils to gain the skills they need in reading and writing. For many of our pupils, the actual skill of decoding may present a barrier. We work hard to remove those barriers so that our children can have as much access to literature as possible.

Pupils benefit from being part of the story. 'Call and respond' is a useful strategy by which pupils can be involved. This may be through vocalising or using sounds, percussion. Single message switches can be used to involve the pupil in a story. St Francis has a multi-interactive learning environment (MILE) room which can be utilised for such experiences. We also have a range of sensory equipment. Stories. rhymes, and singing may also form part of the pupils' swimming experiences. The swimming pool also has multi-sensory equipment. Visiting storytellers have also supported the school.

Pre-formal learners may use objects of reference as a prerequisite to reading.

The key point for our pre-formal learners is personalisation and recognising high engagement activities. For some, this may be through reading and storytelling.

Carla Nicholson, INSPIRE SEND Alliance

Where are we now?

It is useful to conduct an audit around the school environment to ensure that a shared understanding about the importance of reading is reflected in the literacy opportunities offered. Make sure that pupils are immersed in the wonders and curiosity of stories and create excitement and a love for books in their widest sense! I encourage schools to go back to the diagram of foundation skills discussed earlier in the book, as shown in Figure 7.2.

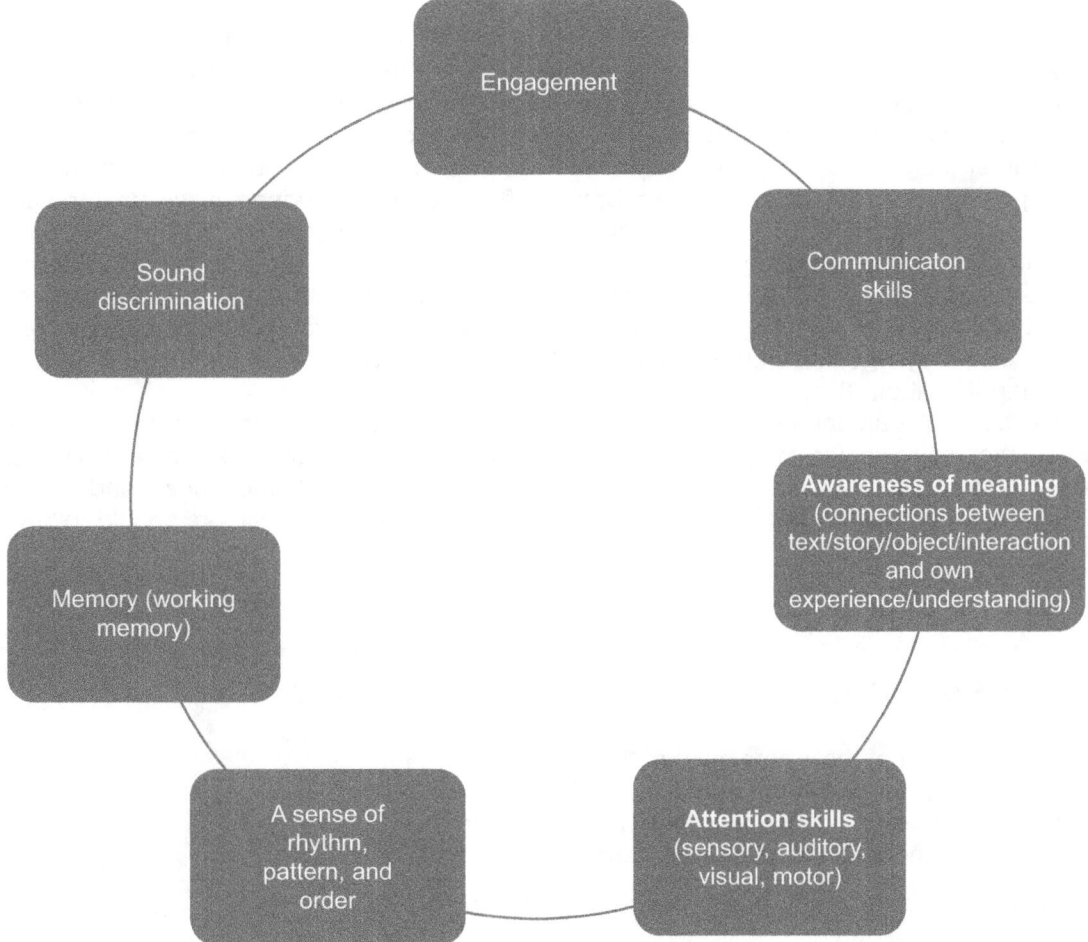

Figure 7.2 Proposed cycle of foundation skills.

By looking at this cycle of skills, which is not exclusive, they are provided with a good starting point and schools can begin to discuss how they currently support learners in each of these areas.

These are all foundation aspects of an inclusive reading framework; we are therefore starting from what is already in place. We can talk about all learners as readers within an inclusive reading framework; each will be on their own personalised path starting and finishing at a different destination. This means everyone is included in the discussion and we can all work together, support, resource, and develop the pathways to ensure that the needs of each learner are being met.

> **Ideas in action: a special school**
>
> **School** – Delamere School, @DelamereSchool
>
> **Context** – Delamere School is a community-maintained specialist primary school for children aged 3–11. We have 110 places with additional nursery provision for children with complex learning needs including learning difficulty, autism, sensory impairments, and developmental delay.
>
> **Intent and Implementation** – The children in EYFS have been exploring the iDinosaur augmented reality book during our reading sessions. We have been using the app on the iPad to make the dinosaurs in the book come to life.
>
> **Impact** – The children responded in lots of ways, such as looking behind the iPad to see if the dinosaur was really there and commenting on what they saw. The book was a great tool for communication, as well as developing pre-reading skills and using technology.

Assessment

It is important to briefly discuss the role of assessment, as it is fundamental to the process of learning. It is important that we know where learners are and their starting points, as well as where we would like them to go. The issue for many learners with complex needs is that assessment can become a tick box exercise and the focus can sometimes be on the outcome rather than the experience. I refer to the clip in my training of the Scottish grandmother reading *The Wonky Donkey* by Craig Smith (2010) to her grandson, www.youtube.com/watch?v=gbsZohEMn38. This is to demonstrate the importance of providing the experiences, opportunities, and rich literacy environments without expecting there to be some form of change or response. The focus is therefore on the process rather than the product. If learners are not offered the opportunity to be immersed in these rich literacy environments, in which exposure to language and print is provided, they do not have the opportunity to develop an understanding about this.

What is useful is an understanding of the learner's strengths, what engagement looks like, the barriers that may exist for learning, and an awareness of the next steps. This enables us to place learners within different aspects of an inclusive reading framework. Koppenhaver and Erickson (2020) propose that we ask the following four questions to decide if learners should follow an emergent literacy pathway or a comprehensive literacy pathway.

> **Does the student**
>
> - Know most of the letters most of the time?
> - Engage actively during shared reading?
> - Have a means of communication and interaction?
> - Understand that writing involves letters and words?
>
> To find out more, read Koppenhaver and Erickson (2020).

Emergent literacy would include our pre-formal and the beginnings of a semi-formal curriculum pathway. All learners would be involved in emergent literacy experiences that include immersion in a rich literary environment. They would have regular access to shared reading and the development of an understanding of the link between language and text through meaningful activities and approaches.

Conventional literacy would focus on more comprehensive structured instruction found within the bulk of our semi-formal and formal curriculum pathways. The CandLE literacy programme developed by Marion Stanton further divides phases into the following

> **The CandLE literacy programme**
>
> **Early emergent** – We do not know if the student has any literacy skills or knowledge, so we just give them some exposure. Do sensory-to-text activities.
>
> **Emergent** – It seems they know some letters or can read their own name. Use predictable chart writing and alternative pencils and start teaching them sounds and whole words.
>
> **Transitioning** – The student knows the letters of the alphabet most of the time and loves stories. Start teaching sounds, whole words, and comprehension.
>
> **Early conventional** – Students being supported to understand and create sentences using whole-word knowledge alongside phonic strategies.
>
> **Developing conventional** – The student is ready to tackle phonics activities and partake in mainstream class activities.
>
> **Conventional** – The student is ready for a conventional English curriculum.
>
> https://candleaac.com/literacyprogramme/
> https://candleaac.com/literacyresourcesforall/

The important aspect here is rather than determining in advance that learners may not be able engage with language and text, we could begin with the assumption that all emergent literacy experiences are relevant to everyone.

Literacy profile

In my training, I discuss the use of a literacy profile. It is a way of building a picture of a learner's skills, ensuring that information about the learner is captured in one place for everyone to access. I recommend a one-page profile related to the learner's literacy skills, focusing on their strengths and what motivates or engages them.

The following box contains some of the key questions I suggest schools think about, ask, and have an awareness of, in relation to learners' literacy understanding. Use this information to inform where a learner's journey within the framework can begin and how the barriers can be reduced.

> - What motivates learners to engage or attend to shared reading activities? (think about the wide range of aspects this could include and who may hold this valuable information.)
> - How do they communicate, and what methods are preferred?
> - How do they access language/print (books, digital text, sensory stories, story massage, immersive experiences, songs, rhymes, raps, drama, making their own books, etc.)
> - What is the preferred method for this? (Low-tech methods, splint's supports, eye gaze, E-tran frames, AAC, switch, laser pointers, recording devices, speech to text, text to speech, QR codes, etc.)
> - Do they have an awareness of sounds around them and differences between them?

> - Do they respond to stories or seek out sounds? Do they enjoy the sounds of words?
> - Can they attend or show awareness of this?
> - Do they have an awareness of rhythm, of pattern or of order?
> - Can they access pictures, objects, print, letters and sounds, or whole words?
> - What is their understanding about print?
> - Consider their access to writing and mark making
> - Are they beginning to recognise letter sounds and to use phonics?
> - Do they have a bank of sight words they are able to recognise?

This information then needs to feed into our framework of monitoring and assessing a learner's engagement and outcomes.

- We need to consider whether there is a framework in place that enables the planning, delivery, monitoring, and assessment of learners' skills and engagement.
- Do we know the barriers that exist and how these can be reduced and access can be promoted? Are we aware of how motivation and engagement can be enhanced by the topic medium or presentation of the activities and strategies used?

Word recognition and language comprehension

Once we have established an understanding about what is in place, we then need to look at opportunities that are provided for learners to access language comprehension and word recognition. Regular opportunities to access these important strands will be influenced by the structures that we have in place – existing frameworks and timetables – alongside an awareness of why it is important to include each of these aspects. This will look different depending on the pathways that learners are on and whether they are accessing a pre-formal, semi-formal, or formal curriculum. We need to go back to the Reading Rope (Figure 7.3) and understand how each of those threads that make up the strands of language comprehension and word recognition reach into the wheel of the foundation skills that all learners are accessing.

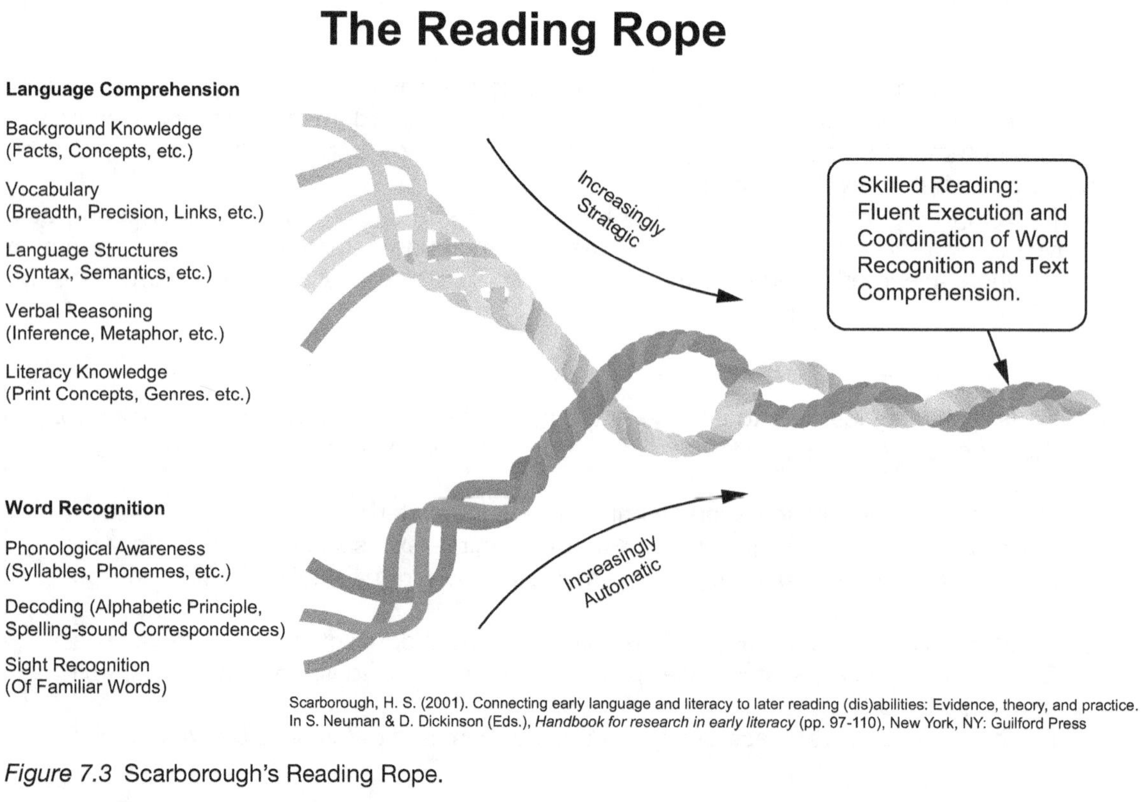

The Reading Rope

Language Comprehension

Background Knowledge (Facts, Concepts, etc.)

Vocabulary (Breadth, Precision, Links, etc.)

Language Structures (Syntax, Semantics, etc.)

Verbal Reasoning (Inference, Metaphor, etc.)

Literacy Knowledge (Print Concepts, Genres, etc.)

Increasingly Strategic

Skilled Reading: Fluent Execution and Coordination of Word Recognition and Text Comprehension.

Word Recognition

Phonological Awareness (Syllables, Phonemes, etc.)

Decoding (Alphabetic Principle, Spelling-sound Correspondences)

Sight Recognition (Of Familiar Words)

Increasingly Automatic

Scarborough, H. S. (2001). Connecting early language and literacy to later reading (dis)abilities: Evidence, theory, and practice. In S. Neuman & D. Dickinson (Eds.), *Handbook for research in early literacy* (pp. 97-110), New York, NY: Guilford Press

Figure 7.3 Scarborough's Reading Rope.

Each curriculum pathway should ensure there are rich literacy opportunities and environments at the heart, so that every learner is getting access to learning about language, sound, and print that surrounds them. This is provided in an engaging, motivating, and accessible way, but it is there, and it is part of the inclusive reading framework. Alongside this rich environment will be opportunities to gain a greater understanding about elements of language comprehension and word recognition.

Four Blocks Literacy Framework

The Four Blocks Literacy Framework is a comprehensive approach to teaching literacy (Cunningham et al., 2008) that has been adapted by Erickson and Koppenhaver for students with disabilities. This forms the basis of the approach used by organisations such as CandLE as well as my own research and consultancy. The Four Blocks model consists of providing learners with the opportunity to access the following four key areas.

1. Guided and shared reading
2. Self-selected reading
3. Working with words
4. Writing

I recommend reading *Comprehensive Literacy for All* by Koppenhaver and Erickson (2020) for further support and information on this area. The emphasis in the book is on a 'literacy for all' approach, whereby we explicitly link print to language and provide opportunities for all learners to become literate (Figure 7.4). There are lots of useful examples of adaptations and structures that will support all aspects of the framework.

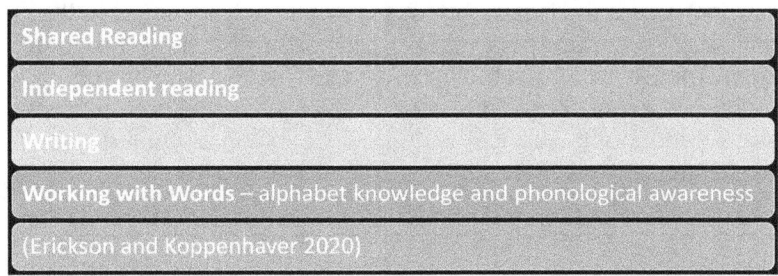

Figure 7.4 Structure of literacy experiences to be offered on a daily or regular basis, according to Erickson and Koppenhaver.

I have started to look in depth at providing opportunities for all learners to be writers/mark makers.

A major challenge in this area is, of course, the aspect of how we define writing for those with significant complex needs. This could form the basis of another book! As with the teaching of reading, the crucial point about the teaching of writing is an assumed competence, where we assign meaning to marks that are made.

For now, I recommend looking at the work of Erickson and Koppenhaver, as well as Jane Farrall's website and blog, she firmly reinforces the view to learners that if you spell it, you can say anything! There are many resources to support this aspect for learners with complex needs, and I have included some useful links in what follows.

> https://literacyforallinstruction.ca/communication/
> www.teachustoo.org.uk/candle-literacy-programme/
> Literacy Resources for All – candleaac.com

www.med.unc.edu/ahs/clds/resources/deaf-blind-model-classroom-resources/predictable-chart-writing/

Caroline Musselwhite (2016): AAC Intervention.com

www.janefarrall.com/teaching-to-the-next-level-using-the-developmental-writing-scale-to-guide-instruction/

Writing Tools: Sensory Pencils and Early Emergent Writers | Jane Farrall Consulting

Regular structured literacy opportunities

Regular structured literacy opportunities are key to an inclusive reading framework. Using our own literacy profile, engagement profiles, and other assessment tools, we will know where learners might be in terms of our curriculum pathway. A diverse learning environment with an exposure to a high/rich level of print, anticipation, and stories should be provided. We should be creative with the use of ICT to motivate and engage all learners.

Consider our access to technology to bring text to life! Use the following.

- Whiteboards
- Interactive floors and surfaces
- Sensory rooms
- Augmentative reality
- Text readers
- Text to speech and speech to text support
- Smart devices
- Tablets, iPads, apps and more

Learners should have the opportunity to interact regularly with language and text, ensuring that multi-sensory approaches are the heart. Activities should include creating their own stories and text, rewriting familiar stories, recording responses, celebrating what has been learnt, creating new and exciting environments, and listening to and interacting with stories, poems, songs, and more, using learners own experiences as a core motivator to ensure engagement and participation. As emphasised throughout, we must widen our definition of what a book is to create more inclusive opportunities for all.

Ideas in action: story sharing

Research shows that personal stories are how we make sense of what happens in our lives – they are central to our sense of who we are.

https://storysharing.org.uk/about/faqs/

- 65–80% of communications relate to a personal experience
- We make and keep friends through sharing stories
- Telling our stories can lead to social change – it is empowering
- The ability to tell a story helps with communication, language, and educational achievement
- Sharing stories helps to build recovery and resilience after difficult times
- Telling stories is creative and fun

Extracts from the Story sharing website, https://storysharing.org.uk/

Sight word learning

If a learner can recognise some words by sight (name, family words, food, etc.), you can begin by developing this bank of sight words known. The key is keeping this personalised and motivating.

What does the learner enjoy? What interests them? The starting point is to make the experience personal to them.

> ### Ideas in action: my experience within a special school
>
> **Context** – I once worked with a young man who was 15 and the staff felt could not read and never would (he had been assessed as a learner with severe learning difficulties). The learner had a very spiky experience of literacy and stories; he was past the age that repetitive books were of interest; he was very aware of things being babyish; he could recognise his name and key words around him. Any form of phonics teaching led to challenging behaviour.
>
> **Intent and Implementation** – The young man wanted to be a mechanic when he left school, so we began creating books about cars, using simple language structures. We used pictures of supercars he loved. Slowly more and more words were recognised, and he began to talk about and share his books with others. Once we have a bank of words he felt confident with, we used initial sounds of words to begin to teach him phonics.
>
> The impact for him was he noticed words around him, he engaged in more reading behaviours, and – over time – developed an understanding of more text.

I am often told by parents and carers that their child is not reading words but remembering them. My response is great – they are becoming a reader! The ability to notice words, to link this to language, and be aware that the text holds meaning is fundamental.

> ### Ideas in action: a special school
>
> **Context** – Jess Norman, teacher at Ash Field Academy. Ashfield is a specialist school catering for pupils from age 4–19. Their key specialism is in ensuring an excellent education for pupils with complex medical conditions or serious physical disabilities in a safe and nurturing environment. The pupil population has a wide range of cognitive ability, from those with profound and multiple learning difficulties (PMLD) to those with more moderate learning difficulties (MLD). In addition to physical and learning needs and disabilities, many pupils also have communication and sensory needs.
>
> **Intent** – To increase pupils access to print in relation meaningful context, starting with awareness of learners' names. The class group contained learners with PMLD.
>
> **implementation** – After becoming aware that some learners recognised their names, staff began to widen the use of names in relation to meaningful activities. They began to use them for the register, paired with photos of the learners.
>
> **Impact** – Learners were able to recognise their names regularly and have now shown an increased interest in the text contained in books. The classroom is now a place where names hold appropriate value.

I encourage schools to look at each of the curriculum pathways and consider our learners being provided with the opportunity to access the following.

1. Rich literacy environment, with accessible and engaging opportunities
2. Opportunities to link language and print
3. Opportunities for repetition, overlearning, and spaced learning
4. Opportunities for multi-sensory learning to provide multiple paths for information to get to the brain (dual coding)

5. Opportunities to review the language level of learners and the impact on their working memory when planning activities (again providing information visually, using auditory information and multi-sensory approaches)
6. Opportunities to ensure barriers to learning have been reduced (e.g., for non-verbal learners, provide opportunities to indicate choice – yes/no cards, same/different cards, iPad, AAC, eye gaze, E-Tran frame)
7. Opportunities for explicit teaching related to decoding, letter name identification, letter sound identification, identifying letters in text, manipulating, segmenting, and blending letter sounds, as well as producing the letter forms.

Using core texts

I recommend lots of interesting and varied text within my training, as it is through access to these that everything else can be linked. By using core engaging and motivating stories, poems, songs, or non-fiction text, you have a way of scaffolding learning for all. It ensures that there is meaning and context running through the learning. You can then provide learners with opportunities to be involved in or experience the text in lots of ways, with multi-sensory approaches at the heart.

In all activities and approaches, consider how to provide accessible opportunities to smoothly link sensory representation to communication/language and text. Do not make it a case of either/or; instead, introduce communication and language with meaningful exposure to environmental print. Learners' understanding of the strands within language comprehension and word recognition can be supported and developed using core text.

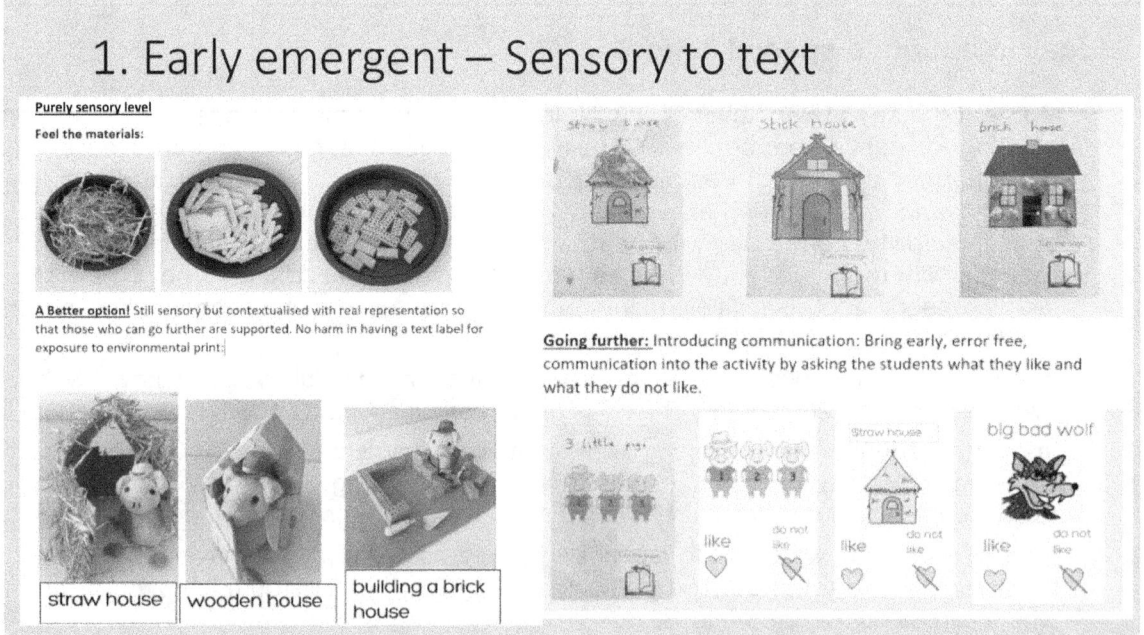

Figure 7.5 Early emergent activities providing a link between sensory experiences and exposure to environmental print (Marion Stanton).

Provide access to text through real books, digital libraries, sensory books and more. Opportunities for assistive technology, as well as accessibility for all should be woven into the design of all activities.

These can include the following (Table 7.1).

Table 7.1 Practical ways into planning for an inclusive reading curriculum

Activity	These help to develop and ways in
Shared reading: provide daily opportunities to share with learner; make sure that these provide a wide range of high-quality texts that are familiar and are different than the experiences and perspective of all learners	A love and joy of reading.
	Hearing learners read and sharing books is key to ensuring a literacy-rich experience.
	Vocabulary/meaning attached to stimulus – supports an understanding that words carry meaning.
	Book handling – develops an understanding of sequence, start, finish, shared interaction.
	Provides a range of vocabulary, language, and repetition.
	Provides opportunities to develop second-tier vocabulary (that pupils are unlikely to come across in everyday conversation).
	Recognising letters and sounds opportunities to model and practise combining sounds.
	Read and share stories, poems, and text, whereby you encourage learners to anticipate, predict, and talk about events.
	Read together in real context (timetables, days of the week, names, bus timetable, shopping list, menu, signs when out in the community), create group stories, use daily communication opportunities.
Guided reading: using activities whereby all learners share the same book, story sack/sensory story	This provides a bridge between independent and shared reading, enabling shared learning, and experiences of language are scaffolded and reinforced.
	Connections are made between text and language.
Create own stories to use, or comic strips, recipes, etc.	Experiences such as sensory stories ensure that learners understand meanings from everything they hear through sensory representations.
Independent reading: create acceptable opportunities for learners to explore and experience text	This supports a greater degree of choice-making.
	Time to explore text and language (iPads, AAC, accessible book formats).
	Consider how learners can have these opportunities (use online stories, non-fiction text, poems, and songs, whilst turning on subtitles to reinforce language heard).
	Use ways to encourage reading aloud (e.g., online programmes such as www.fonetti.com), recording own stories, smart speakers.
Drama and immersive experiences	Bring language to life.
	Make literacy accessible to all learners.
	Enable them to be part of it and develop anticipation, self-awareness, and fun!
	Approaches such as 'call and response' (Park, 2012) can bring literature such as Shakespeare to life for learners at all ages and stages!
	It is important to teach literacy alongside communication.
	http://thinkingtalking.co.uk/;
	www.projectcore
Storytelling and the creation of personalised books or own books	Narrative and storytelling are hugely powerful tools for all learners.
	Develop opportunities to share stories and experiences within and around us.
	Provide opportunities to create personalised representations based on experiences, e.g. personalised story boxes, boards, talkers, books and sacks, and life quilts based on the learner's interests and experiences.
	Use photos to generate pictures for text, books to read and write – use images of themselves laughing, having fun, and fully engaged in an activity.

(*Continued*)

Table 7.1 (Continued)

Activity	These help to develop and ways in
	Books can range from a simple picture cut from a magazine – with one word or a simple sentence – to a more complex book made on the iPad and shared on the whiteboard.
	Books can be a sequence of images on a large piece of paper, objects in a box, or contained in a multi-pocket plastic wallet for taking home and sharing.
	Sensory stories, bags/boxes, story maps, sensory massage, and more are brilliant ways in for all.
	These can be extended from storytelling through objects or pictures to words.
	Use technology whiteboards and sounds made by learners to capture and create texts, e.g., "we need to laugh", "we need to eat", "we need to smile", "we need to talk", "we need to listen".
	Use familiar book formats to create similar structured text. Use words that create simple sentences from the start. For example, "I like . . . ", "I see . . . ", "red car/blue car", etc.
	Make sure learners can read/understand words from the beginning.
	Build up a bank of words known; celebrate how many a learner can read. Record on a chart, keep in a box or special bag, and continue to share and talk about them as readers.
	Teaching language in a fun and memorable way, repeating accessible information and language looking at its features and patterns.

Provide all learners with opportunities for overlearning and repetition. There are many strategies that will be useful to support learners including games (matching, finding), digital and real apps, and strategies such as precision teaching, etc. It is important to consider how this will look for each learner in terms of their stage and age. Continue to create an interest in vocabulary and language (e.g., Vocabulary Ninja's word of the day at https://vocabularyninja.co.uk/word-of-the-day/). All of this is important for any learner to support the transfer of information to long-term memory.

The teaching of phonics

I have added this next section as a separate part, due to the discussion and confusion about how phonics fits into an inclusive reading framework. The teaching of phonics is a key aspect of decoding, as discussed in the previous chapter. The foundations of this are rooted in the development of an awareness of the difference and meaning of sound. Remember that when you are teaching something new within this area, it is important to go back to foundation skills. If you are on a semi-formal pathway, maybe learning about digraphs (how two graphemes combine to make one phoneme), the foundations for learning should be focused on sound discrimination within an engaging context.

Pre-formal curriculum pathway

If learners are accessing a pre-formal curriculum pathway, learning will be centred on the cycle of foundation skills with opportunities to experience how language and text relate to each other. This will occur through communication activities, musical opportunities, and multi-sensory experiences. Learners will be submerged in a literacy-rich environment whereby shared reading and print referencing will be part of the everyday curriculum. Through this, they will have the opportunity to experience and become aware of letters and sounds, within a meaningful context as part of their existing environment. There should be lots of opportunities to experience language (communicate in its widest sense), learn about sound, and listen/experience sound in relation to vocabulary and the sounds in words.

Semi-formal curriculum pathway

This is where a more structured approach to the teaching of phonics is used. As you move into a semi-formal pathway, learners continue to experience regular speaking and listening activities that are well matched to their developing abilities and interests. They are given the opportunity to develop an awareness of the link between speech and the sounds within words. Learners should be provided with opportunities to connect letters to sounds and develop awareness of grapheme-phoneme correspondence. This requires the inclusion of activities that involve blending and segmenting the sounds in words, opportunities to develop an awareness of differences between sounds (through alliteration, segmentation, blending, and rhyming), and opportunities to tune into speech sounds.

It is important to ensure access for all learners to decodable readers (books in the widest sense) that support learners' stage and progress. It is crucial at this stage to continuously assess the teaching of phonics, as complex psycho-linguistic skills are involved, alongside a good working memory, aspects that may be compromised for learners with complex needs.

Ideas in action: case study from a special school

School – Joanne Worrall, Coppice school, Doncaster.

Context – 130 pupils aged 3–19 years with severe learning difficulties and autism.

Intent and Implementation – Originally using 'letters and sounds', we adapted the order in which the phonemes and graphemes were taught to align with the developmental order of speech sounds and removed the need to introduce 'nonsense' words to our pupils, as there was no meaning behind them and comprehension at single word level was an area in which our pupils needed more support. We then purchased 'Essential Letters and Sounds' (ELS), as it closely followed the principles and teaching sequence outlined in the original 'letters and sounds' document, which meant fewer overall changes for our staff and pupils; in addition, it was free of jargon and focused on whole-class sessions.

We have three paces at which letter sounds are taught, depending on the ability of the learner to remember and retain the information and the degree of overlearning they require. We have three options for lesson delivery. The removal of year groups and terms in which the graphemes are to be taught allows for opportunities for overlearning and for any phase to be taught across school to link with their developmental stage, not their chronological age.

We remove 'nonsense' words and use a combined approach from different strategies. Blank level questioning is used to support comprehension skills, PECS are used to support word-level understanding and develop communication skills and sensory stories delivered repeatedly, as with the principles from 'Talk for Writing' (www. talk4writing.com), to develop engagement and anticipation of stories and story language through repeated sensory input.

Impact – With the adoptions and changes we have made, we are seeing the benefits. We believe there is a place for phonics within a specialist setting; the repetitive nature and familiar structure within phonics sessions, feeding into the limbic system's need for routine, will become a 'safe' and familiar activity, keeping neurological pathways open and developing engagement, learning, and progress.

What to consider when choosing a structured synthetic phonics programme (SSP)

Current approaches to the teaching of reading within the UK emphasise the use of an SSP as recommended within the reading framework (DfE, 2021). In my experience, I have used a variety of approaches to the teaching of phonics. These have included top-down approaches (such as analytic phonics) and bottom-up approaches (such as synthetic phonics). The difference between these is that a top-down approach begins with the whole word and then moves to the phonemes and graphemes. A bottom-up approach begins with the phonemes and graphemes, then builds up to make whole words. There is also an approach referred to as linguistic phonics (McGuinness, 2006), whereby the progression is from sounds made in speech to print. The focus is on teaching learners to crack the print code and be aware of how different sounds are represented by letters. Some linguistic approaches fall under the heading of synthetic phonics programmes, whilst others may not. During my training, I recommend looking at the programme developed by Ann Sullivan (2018) called Phonics for Pupils with Special Educational Needs and reading her blog www.phonicsforpupilswithspecialeducationalneeds.com/blog.

Fidelity to one structured synthetic phonics approach is advocated within the reading framework (DfE, 2021). I recommend to schools that whatever approach they decide to use, there should be regular opportunities to monitor and review the progress of learners. It is only then that further decisions can be made about the appropriateness of the approach and next steps.

Currently, there is no preferred SSP programme or approach by Ofsted. The guidance is that whatever approach is used, it must be rigorous, systematic, and used with fidelity (DfE, 2021). Approaches differ in relation to terminology such as actions, mnemonics, prompts, keywords, and routines to teach knowledge and skills. We know that for learners with complex needs, there is no aspect of the curriculum or learning process where one size fits all learners. Therefore, why would it be considered that one approach to a very specialised aspect of reading will meet the needs of all learners with complex needs? A positive outcome of this emphasis is that special schools are looking more closely at the curriculum they are providing for their learners in terms of the teaching of reading.

The questions being asked are the following.

- What are current methods for teaching learners to read?
- Are they appropriate?
- Do they provide learners with the best opportunities to develop an understanding between language and text?

If one approach to teaching phonics is used, schools should consider

- Will it support those learners working at a slower pace?
- Are there appropriate adaptations or provisions for a range of needs?
- Does this affect fidelity?
- Are there enough books, activities, and resources to support learners who remain in specific stages for many years/forever?

This requires discussion, negotiation, clarity around pathways, and agreement across schools and providers.

Points to remember when teaching phonics

- Consider the scope and sequence of your lessons in terms of introducing GPC
- Think about visually and auditory similar GPCs
- Consider introducing the most useful letters and sounds first
- Use a small set and build gradually – single letters and sounds before diagraphs and trigraphs

- Consider the number of sounds that are taught each week, although we need to slow this down to support our learners; one per week may not be enough to hold interest and engagement
- Consider using three to five sounds per week – make sure this is supported by assessment of the learner's progress and engagement
- This must be supported by the GPCs that are contained within the decodable readers used (consider making own readers)
- Make explicit links between print and speech; encourage generalised understanding from the beginning rather than rote learning of specific GPC in isolation from text and meaning
- For all learners, there should be a consistent scope and sequence across the school; if there is no success after a few weeks, go back to earlier more inclusive approaches, developing awareness of differences between sounds

Whatever approach is used

All approaches to teaching reading should provide learners with the opportunities to develop awareness of the link between language and print across all areas of their curriculum. Remember the teaching of phonics is one aspect of the teaching of reading. It is useful to include some of the following aspects at meaningful opportunities.

- Point out letters and print in the environment
- Talk about letters and their sounds when you encounter them in everyday activities
- Use oral segmenting and blending in games (Play 'I Spy')
- Use mirrors modelling, intensive interaction, and feeling and looking at how sounds are made with our mouths (use recordable mirror tiles)
- Provide opportunities to play with letter shapes and sounds
- Explicitly reference letter names and sounds in shared reading and writing activities
- Explicitly teach, model, and emphasise sounds and letters throughout the day in meaningful contexts
- Teach phonological skills during all activities (e.g. read aloud, telling stories, writing activities, word work, predictable chart writing, guided reading)
- Connect to word meaning – connect to word webs
- Sound matching and sorting activities can be done with devices, PODD (Pragmatic Organisation Dynamic Display, way of organising vocabulary in communication such as a communication book), eye-gaze frames and with low tech paper solutions
- Use mnemonics and actions
- Use multi-sensory approaches (see the sound, feel the sound, make the sound)
- Reinforce, repeat, and provide opportunities to develop and consolidate learning throughout their educational career.
- Remember this process is a journey and learners will begin this at different points and the destination continuously shifts.
- None of us will ever consider ourselves as having learnt to read every word and text that exists; it is a lifelong journey for all of our learners who deserve to be part of this.

Ideas in action: case study from a special school

School – Andy Heywood, teacher at a Durham special school educating pupils 2–19 years of age, with autism or profound, moderate, severe, or complex learning difficulties. Some pupils also have additional medical, physical, sensory, linguistic, or behavioural difficulties. Each pupils has an EHCP.

Context – We have 240 pupils and 120 staff. We provide a further education unit (FEU – Post 16) on site up to 19 years of age. My class is a 14–19 specialist ASD provision with emphasis on being a further education unit. All pupils have a diagnosis of ASD with some with a diagnosis of Down's syndrome. No pupils in the class exceed Year 2 standard, with some pupils at YN standard.

Intent – To increase access a structured literacy approach.

Implementation – I identified each of the communication styles of pupils in the class and have started individual plans to implement Makaton, use of symbols, PECS (a unique alternative/augmentative communication system), etc. All pupils now receive daily alphabetic/phonics lessons personalised to need. Reading is incorporated into regular sessions linked to real-life experiences, e.g., "The Tunnel" linked to a visit to a park that had various types of tunnels and exploring these in a sensory way. Comprehension developed by implementing Blanks Questioning Levels 1–4 and adapting this across all focus areas. All staff in class base received CPD regarding the teaching of reading and the approaches taken within it. Identification of assessment procedures are in place using Blanks/Cherry Gardens (Blank levels assessment for speech and language (https://www.southwestyorkshire.nhs.uk/wp-content/uploads/2020/08/Blank-questioning-information.pdf) / Cherry Garden assessment Framework (https://tapestry.info/features/cherry-garden.html).

Impact – I now have more confidence with all learners; they are vocalising more and are keen to improve their alphabetic and phonic knowledge. They have reduced identified gaps in learning and are keen to use their method of communication more freely and willingly. Students previously identified as non-verbal are using alphabetical sounds, and I believe that they are feeling increasingly safe to experiment with sounds and words. The impact on social, emotional and mental health (SEMH) and emotional welfare is huge. I am just loving the difference and engagement. The impact has been felt on professional development school-wide, and it has influenced the direction of the development of reading in the school.

Time for reflection

Consider how you promote partnership working between home and school.

Are approaches to literacy that are used at home and at school clearly shared and understood?

How could this be further promoted?

References

Cunningham, P., Hall, D. & Sigmon, C. (2008) *The Teacher's Guide to the Four-Blocks Literacy Model Published by Four Blocks*. Greensboro, NC: Four Blocks.

Department for Education. (2021) *The reading framework: Teaching the foundations of literacy* [online] Available at: www.gov.uk/government/publications/the-reading-framework-teaching-the-foundations-of-literacy [Accessed: 23/06/2022]

Koppenhaver, D. & Erickson, K. (2020) *Comprehensive Literacy for All: Teaching Students with Significant Disabilities to Read and Write*. Baltimore, MD: Paul H. Brookes Publishing Co.

McGuinness, D. (2006) *Early Reading Instruction: What Science Really Tells Us about How to Teach Reading*. Cambridge, MA: MIT Press.

Park, K. (2012) *TRANSCRIPT: Call and Response*.

Smith, C. (2010) *The Wonky Donkey*. New York.

Sullivan, A. (2018) *Phonics for Pupils with Special Educational Needs: Building Basics: Introducing Sounds and Letters*. Abingdon, UK: Routledge.

Conclusion

In the final few words of this book, I want to pull together some of the main ideas and approaches I have suggested. This book was written to provide some guidance based on my experience, rather than provide all the answers. The process of learning to read is a complex one, and I have spent many years trying to find a clear path to support the learners I have worked with. Throughout the book I have suggested that we begin by:

1. Focusing on how we learn to read, looking at the skills, experiences, and opportunities that we need to provide to support learners
2. Focusing on reducing barriers to learning and increasing motivation and engagement

Focusing on how we learn to read

As summed up by Such (2022) in his blog,

> *Reading is the comprehension of visual symbols that represent spoken language. To do this, pupils must develop two capacities that become increasingly integrated as expertise develops – (1) recognising words, and (2) building meaning from those words.*

It is our role to provide the opportunities, experiences, and environment to give all learners the chance to become readers in the widest sense. To support word recognition, we need to provide lots of opportunities to associate language with its meaning and link this to objects, pictures, and print. To support language comprehension and the building of meaning, we need to provide meaningful and engaging experiences with rich language opportunities. There are a number of key strategies that we can use to support all learners, as follow.

Create a rich literacy environment

Immerse learners in the wonders and curiosity of stories – create excitement, enjoyment, and a love of language. Create a rich, diverse, and engaging literacy environment from an early age that contains lots of experiences of language (talk, talk, and more talk), vocabulary, sounds, stories, drama, music, songs, rhymes, books of all kinds (including text represented through sensory stories, story boxes, e books, audio books, and more!), puppets, and print. Check out *Sensory Stories to Support Additional Needs: Making Narratives Accessible Through the Senses* by Joanna Grace (2022) for some inspiration. Provide experience of and surround with, real books and technology to ensure access for all.

> **Ideas in action: a sensory story**
>
> **"Lolli Ladybird's Got Spots" by Pete Wells**
>
> (Author of Inclusive Stories, host of the Sensory Stories Podcast)
>
> **Context** – Catcote Futures Specialist College in Hartlepool caters to learners with high needs between the ages of 19 and 25. This is a story about a ladybird who goes to see

the doctor after noticing she has large black spots on her shell! In the waiting room, there are other minibeasts who are worried about their perceived illnesses (a snail who is very slow, a wasp who is always angry). At the end, the doctor informs them they are all normal and their features make them who they are.

Intent – Differs depending on individual outcomes of learners, cohorts of learners/ implementation strategies used. When delivering the story to some of my PMLD learners, the intent is to tolerate touch, or increase engagement or co-active exploration, to work on cause-and-effect skills, whilst for another, it was to use functional communication eye pointing to answer simple questions or make choices. With all of these learners, I was looking for toleration and recognition of props, anticipation of favoured items, exploration of the props leading to functional exploration, and even coactive play.

For my complex needs cohort, I am looking for fleeting interaction with props, matching symbol to symbol or symbol to item and simple sentence creation. The sentence building group included a young man who had a voice output communication aid (VOCA) and was using this to create simple sentences from a bespoke grid. Another learner was matching character to character as the story went along and in the centre of the room was a container filled with the creatures from the story which learners would find. For my learners with autism, the intent is to promote interaction between peers, understanding of emotions and emotional regulation (through the zones of regulation), employing communication skills, and addressing anxieties around going to see the doctor.

For my SLD cohort, I was looking for an understanding of diversity and acceptance of who they are. Positive self-esteem and good SEMH are significant drivers, and this story was designed to empower learners. Intent for all was to practice vital early literacy, communication, and calculation skills.

Impact – For my PMLD cohort, I saw retention of skills and application of skills in wider contexts (for example, one learner really enjoyed the ball we used and would initiate interaction through gesture and eye pointing). The ball was a prop in the next story we did, and I saw a more immediate response to this prop, as well as increased anticipation and engagement.

With the learners with autism, engagement with the zones of regulation was high, helping to cement a common language to sensitively express feelings and anxieties. The learners were encouraged to explore props with their peers, with much success.

Finally, with my SLD cohort, learners were able to show progress in functional reading and evidence of building of simple sentences when answering comprehension questions and completing a range of paper-based activities. SEMH issues were discussed more openly and sensitively, and self-worth and peer relationships were enhanced through positive activities that promoted kindness and friendship.

So one simple story, delivered through a variety of methods to a wide range of learners, resulted in a significant amount of impact. Not bad for an under-confident little ladybird! If you want a copy, go to https://sensorystoriespodcast.com/podcast-files/ or subscribe to Inclusive Technology's Inclusive Stories (www.helpkidzlearn.com/shop/online-software/inclusive-stories) for a truly beautiful version of the story!

High expectations

Reading is everywhere. We need to create routines to make it part of everyday life, reading for information, independence, and pleasure. Read aloud or hear stories at least daily, making it an active, fun experience whereby learners are read with rather than to using whatever medium supports them, e.g., big books, sensory stories, story mats, and all forms of ICT. Talk about stories, poems, text, question, reflect, predict, and share ideas. Simply reading to learners has a huge impact and creates new neural networks in the brain, leading to deeper learning and understanding. Include reading within curriculum frameworks, timetables, support with ideas in action on websites, and in our discussions about all learners journeys.

Ideas in action: Amy's story

Amy, who was born in 2003, was starved of oxygen, which resulted in brain damage. The undisputed fact, however, was that Amy would have very complex needs – and although some professionals had hope, the majority believed Amy incapable of any progress.

At the age of 6, Amy started to attend a special needs school where they follow a sensory curriculum. She spent the next six years doing art and craft activities and feeling different objects. No attempt to teach reading, writing, or maths was made, but then Amy had no means of communication and was labelled as having PMLD.

Various speech and language therapists came and went; they tried hand-activated switches, Makaton, symbol cards, objects of reference, smells of reference, and facially activated switches, but all with no success to communicate successfully with Amy. Throughout this time, Amy's dad had been convinced that if he blinked whilst looking at Amy, she would repeat back the blink, and he started experimenting with differing numbers of blinks and eventually we decided to take two quick blinks in succession as a "yes" and a refusal to blink as a "no". Finally, we were able to communicate with Amy in a meaningful way, and we soon discovered she knew what she wanted or needed.

Through establishing a "yes" and "no" response from Amy, it became clear that she could understand what was being said to her. A speech book for Amy to communicate with via "yes" and "no" answers was introduced in 2017 and I started asking for a more formal approach to Amy's education because I believed that she wanted to learn about the world. School tried, but subjects were taught through massage or messy play and were repeated every week for a whole term at a time.

In 2018, Amy and I watched Jonathan's documentary *My Life – Locked in Boy* on television, which had a profound effect on us. I asked Amy if she would like to learn to read and I lost count of how many times she blinked to say "YES!!"

I approached school to ask if they could start to teach Amy to read but was told that they had no experience of teaching children with complex needs and would not know where to start. I approached speech and language therapists but was told they did not teach literacy, only communication. I decided to teach Amy myself and started with Jolly Phonics because that was how Amy's younger brother had been taught to read at mainstream school. Amy appeared very engaged but due to her disabilities could not make the sounds or perform the actions that were required. A different approach was needed, and a friend suggested trying Read Write Inc.

It is important to note here that the label given to Amy of PMLD was interpreted to mean that she had a learning disability, and this was associated with developmental delay; however, it is better to refer to Amy as having learning difficulties because it is her ability to access the learning that is the problem – not that she is incapable of learning.

Amy started to show that she could recognise letters. School continued with the sensory curriculum but gradually allowed Amy more and more time out of the classroom with her carers to work on her reading. It became clear that Amy preferred her lessons with her carers, and I asked if school could start teaching Amy some simple lessons from the national curriculum.

During COVID, home schooling and support of an employed teacher after eight weeks of home schooling Amy read her first book *My Dog Ned* on her own. Her teacher simply turned the pages with Amy indicating through blinks when she had finished a page. She was then asked a series of questions and she answered them all correctly!

Amy's literacy journey started a long time ago. There have been many false starts and setbacks, many obstacles put in her path, and a great deal of incorrect assumptions made – but, without one small step leading to another, we could not have got to where we are now. There is so much more left of this journey, as I strongly believe that it is Amy's dream to be able to eventually spell out the words that she chooses to say and hopefully one day she will have that voice – just like Jonathan.

Every child deserves an education, no matter what their perceived obstacle to learning is, and it is the job of the educationalists to unlock that potential; but without encouragement, guidance, new thinking, belief, and case studies, it can be difficult for some professionals to make that leap from the old traditional ways. It is time to change the thinking of the old-school experts. The possibilities are endless.

Written by Iona Mayo Amy's mum

For the full story of Amy's journey, visit www.teachustoo.org.uk/amy

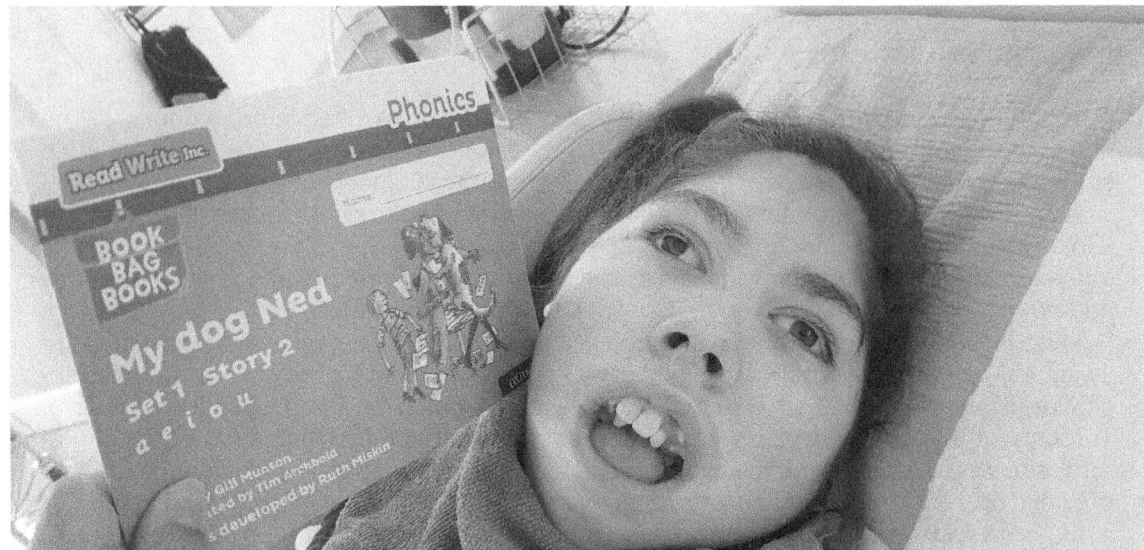

Figure 8.1 Amy and one of the books she can now read.

Integrate accessibility into everything we do

Ensure that learning is multi-sensory, motivating, and accessible, and that it brings stories and text to life (see, hear, feel, touch, taste, and move). Make the most of technology and accessibility add-ons (Book Creator, iPad apps, stories online, scanning pens, text to speech, and more!). Through shared reading opportunities (reading in its broadest sense), we scaffold learning, enabling young people to explore and experience the world through their senses and minds.

Create personalised learning opportunities

Remember to make it meaningful and create opportunities for everyone to be story tellers and develop narrative skills, and make their own books (low and high tech). Always start from where the learner is, building on existing knowledge, strengths, and interests. When learners struggle, go back to skills they were confident with. For example, if learners find moving on to blending in phonics, then go back and consolidate learning at the previous initial sound or foundation skill stage. Remember to include references to print within meaningful contexts.

Repetition and active participation are key!

Young children request the same book many times over. We must create accessible opportunities for our learners to do the same. We will be bored before them! Keep it consistent, positive, and fun, and go at the pace of the learner. It is important to always encourage participation and engagement. The most effective shared reading strategies are those where interaction is enhanced. Jane Farrall has some great ideas on her website and blog to support this including her 'Great Eight' poster (Figure 8.2).

Home–school engagement

The final crucial element to the development of reading for learners with complex needs, is the communication and connection between home and school. It is important that we create

Shared reading: It's all about the interaction

THE GREAT EIGHT

1. SHARE THE AIR
A = Attention Getter
I = Invite Participation
R = Respond or model a response

2. LINK TO LETTERS
Refer to letters in the student's names, or other important letters, when you see them on a page.

3. CROWD TO INVITE PARTICIPATION
Comment on what the students seem to be interested in and wait at least 5 seconds; Invite participation using the different parts of CROWD and wait at least 5 seconds; Respond to whatever the student says/does by adding more language, modeling appropriate grammar.

Completion
Recall
Open ended
Wh- questions
Distancing

4. MODEL "I HAVE A QUESTION"
When you ask a question, explicitly model saying "I have a question," using AAC and then ask it

5. TEACH VOCABULARY
Teach new vocabulary by briefly defining it. You can use synonyms or put the new word in a sentence.

6. DO YOU HAVE A QUESTION?
Ask the students if they have any questions after sharing every 3-4 pages.

7. PRINT REFERENCING
Point out elements of the book as you read it e.g. This is the title of the book. It tells us....

8. RHYMES AND SOUNDS
Point out rhyming words and word plays in texts - words with the same initial letters or which have similar sounds in them (alliteration).

DON'T FORGET
- Sometimes we need to teach students to enjoy books
- Use the student's interests as a starting point if needed
- In shared reading, always model using the student's communication system
- Reading a book repeatedly is great - and important to do!
- The student selects the book when reading 1:1

Figure 8.2 The 'Great Eight' interactive reading strategies, by Jane Farrall.

an environment whereby home and school are working together. Everyone needs to have the opportunity to develop their understanding and be part of the journey. It is the families and carers who hold the inside knowledge. It is fundamental that we work together and share views, and feelings, and celebrate successes. On one of my recent courses, we asked for the views of parents and carers in terms of what aspects they would like to be addressed during the training. Following are some of the interesting responses.

- My child can read aloud, but in school it is felt that children with complex needs cannot understand what they read. How can I help him to demonstrate his understanding?
- How can I engage my child in more than just messy play when they are at home?
- How can I support my son in residential and promote his literacy?
- How can I help my daughter who is bored and can do more than just choose between two objects?
- How can I support my child in literacy?

There are several ways that we can support a link between home and school, and develop reading and literacy awareness across both contexts. These include the following.

- Provide opportunities for learners to take home literacy experiences to share/bring back to school (news activities using symbols, AAC, BIGmack Communicator and recordable devices to support, provide big books, story boxes/sacks, sensory stories, reading books, and more).
- Use QR codes to share digital libraries as well as own made books; encourage this to be used at home, too.
- Model and share approaches that engage learners in both home and school contexts.
- Develop clear communication and opportunities to share information (newsletters, websites, text messaging, home school updates, videos, recorded information).
- Provide workshops and opportunities for parents and carers to showcase their successes and strengths, as well as learn new approaches and strategies.
- Involve parents and carers in activities whereby resources may be made or jointly produced; this should include the creation of interfaces and grids for technology, including AAC.

Finally, it is important to consider how activities and experiences can be integrated into family life. We do not want to impose specific strategies or ideas onto families, but rather work in partnership.

I recommend reading Eye Can Write by Jonathan Bryan 2019. The book explores the journey to becoming literate of Jonathan and his family. Chantal Bryan (Jonathan's mum) emphasises that the path ahead of Jonathan and his family has never been clear or easy (Bryan 2019).

We need to provide a clear path for our families to support all learners to navigate the literacy journey and be aware of what riches lie ahead of them. Above all, make sure that learners are immersed in the wonders and curiosity of stories and create excitement and a love for books.

Throughout this book, there are case studies of learners with complex needs who have demonstrated a wide range of behaviours and skills as a result of a structured and rich literacy environment and opportunities. It is important that we continue to gather examples of this impact upon pupils and encourage there to be an increase in research within this area. There are many positives to developing an inclusive reading framework, and hopefully the examples contained in this book provide the foundation for us to continue to develop opportunities for all of our learners to be part of this!

References

Bryan, J. (2019) *Eye Can Write: A Memoir of a Child's Silent Soul Emerging.* London: Blink Publishing.

Grace, J. (2022) *Sensory Stories to Support Additional Needs: Making Narratives Accessible Through the Senses.* London: Jessica Kingsley Publishers.

Such, C. (2022) *The art and science of teaching primary reading . . . in 500 words* [blog], July 26 Available at: https://primarycolour.home.blog/2022/07/26/500-words/?fbclid=IwAR1SmvEfpYbhzQmCVy9eQ6wOfx138X7B8Ja5P7e6R1ZEkWSKEEaldk_T8sE [Accessed: 24/07/2022]

Index

Note: Page numbers in *italic* indicate a figure and page numbers in **bold** indicate a table on the corresponding page.

accessibility 25, 31–32, 42–45, *43–44*, 106; and assistive technology 45–49; creating collections 41–42; creating digital libraries 45; creating environments 39–40; creating and sharing language 49; and high-quality text 40–41; and the importance of language 32–33; and making your own books 34–39; and sharing stories 33–34; where learners will read 49–51
accessible text 39–40
active participation 106
alphabet books 41
assessment 25, 90–91
assistive technology 45–49, *46*, *48*
audio tapes 41
auditory awareness/sound discrimination 62, 68, 70
auditory pathways 39, *73*
augmented reality texts 42
awareness: auditory 62; of meaning 61; phonological 67–69, *68*

bag books 42
beginning 66–67; building blocks 24–29; and an inclusive view of reading 21–29, 87–88
books: bag books 42; making your own books 34–39, *36*, 41; picture books 41; reference books 42; story books 41
building blocks: inclusive reading framework 24–29, *24*

CandLE literacy programme 91
case studies: and accessible literacy-rich environments 32–35, 39–40, 42–45, 50, 51; and difficulty learning to read 83–84; family 7–8; and high expectations 22, 23–24, 26, 28; and planning 99–100, 102; and phonics 66, 70–71, 74–75; and prioritising reading 3, 15–16, 17; and reading development 53–54, 63
classes: reading spines for 40–41
classrooms 49–51, *50*; *see also* environments, literacy-rich
collections 41–42
comics 41
communication skills 61
community 34
compact discs 41
complex needs, learners with 57–58, *57*, 65–66; and auditory discrimination 70; and the importance of sound 69–70; and orthographic mapping 74–76; and phonics 67, 72–74, 76; and phonological awareness 67–69; and a rich literacy environment 70–72; where to begin 66–67
comprehension *see* language comprehension
Corbett, Pie 34, 40, 55
core texts 96–98
curriculum: curriculum pathways at a special school 13; and literacy 14–18; pre-formal *12*, 99; semi-formal 99–100; *see also* inclusive reading curriculum

decodable text 41
difficulty learning to read: and four stages of processing 79–82; and the use of symbols 83–84
digital libraries 42, 45
digital media opportunities 41

engagement 60–61; engagement model 13–14, *13–14*; engaging text 39–40; home–school engagement 106–108
environments, literacy-rich 24, 31–32, 42–45, 70–72, 103–104; and assistive technology 45–49; creating collections 41–42; creating digital libraries 45; creating environments 39–40; creating and sharing language 49; and high-quality text 40–41; and the importance of language 32–33; and making your own books 34–39; and sharing stories 33–34; where learners will read 49–51
expectations *see* high expectations

family: case study 7–8; home–school engagement 106–108
fiction 41
foundation skills 58–63, *59–60*, *63*, 65–66, **89**; and auditory discrimination 70; and the importance of sound 69–70; and orthographic mapping 74–76; and phonics 67, 72–74, 76; and phonological awareness 67–69; and a rich literacy environment 70–72; where to begin 66–67
Four Blocks Literacy Framework 93–94

graphic novels 41
'Great Eight' interactive reading strategies *107*

high expectations 104–105; building blocks 24–29; and an inclusive view of reading 21–29
high-frequency words 73
high-quality text 40–41
home–school engagement 106–108

ideas in action: Amy's story 105; curriculum pathways at a special school 13; examples from a special school 41; "The Queen's Jubilee" 38; sensory story 103–104; sound, importance of 69–70; special schools 90, 95; story sharing 94; *see also* case studies
impact: defined 11
implementation: defined 11
inclusion: building blocks needed to create an inclusive reading framework 24–29, *24*; inclusive view of reading 21–24; *see also* inclusive reading curriculum
inclusive reading curriculum **97–98**; and assessment 90–91; choosing a structured synthetic phonics programme 100–102; developing a shared understanding 88–89; and the Four Blocks Literacy Framework 93–94; and literacy profile 91–92; pre-formal curriculum pathway 99; and regular structured literacy opportunities 94; semi-formal curriculum pathway 99–100; and sight word learning 94–96; and the teaching of phonics 98; and using core texts 96–98; where to begin 87–88; where are we now 89–90; word recognition and language comprehension 92–93
information gathering 15, 55
information sharing 15
input 80–81
integration 81
intent: defined 11
interactive reading strategies *107*
interests: readings spines for 40–41

key stages: reading spines for 40–41

language: comprehension 25, 92–93; create and share across the school 49; importance of 32–33
learning disabilities: definitions 2
libraries *see* digital libraries
literacy 31–32, 42–45; and assistive technology 45–49; CandLE literacy programme 91; creating collections 41–42; creating digital libraries 45; creating environments 39–40; creating and sharing language 49; and the curriculum framework 14–18; Four Blocks Literacy Framework 93–94; and high-quality text 40–41; and the importance of language 32–33; and making your own books 34–39; profile 91–92; provide opportunities to bring literacy to life 51; regular structured literacy opportunities 25, 94; rich literacy environment 24; and sharing stories 33–34; teaching the foundations of 12; where learners will read 49–51
"Lolli Ladybird's Got Spots" (sensory story) 103–104

mapping *see* orthographic mapping
meaning, awareness of 61
memory 62–63, 81–82
motivation 60–61
multi-sensory approaches 15–17, 35–39, 69–70, 80–82, 94–96

non-fiction 41

opportunities: to bring literacy to life 51; high-quality text as a basis for 40–41; personalised learning 106; regular structured literacy opportunities 25, 94
order 62
orthographic mapping 74–76
output 82
own-made books 41; *see also* books

participation, active 106
pattern 62
personalised learning opportunities 34, 98, 106
phonics 65–66, 76; and auditory discrimination 70; defined 67; and the importance of sound 69–70; and orthographic mapping 74–76; and phonological awareness 67–69; and a rich literacy environment 70–72; structured synthetic phonics programme (SSP) 100–101; teaching of 98; where to begin 66–67; whole word vs. 72–74
phonological awareness 67–69, *68*
picture books 41
planning **97–98**; and assessment 90–91; choosing a structured synthetic phonics programme 100–102; developing a shared understanding 88–89; and the Four Blocks Literacy Framework 93–94; and literacy profile 91–92; pre-formal curriculum pathway 99; and regular structured literacy opportunities 94; semi-formal curriculum pathway 99–100; and sight word learning 94–96; and the teaching of phonics 98; and using core texts 96–98; where to begin 87–88; where are we now 89–90; word recognition and language comprehension 92–93
plays 41
policy *see* reading policy
pop-up books 42
pre-formal curriculum *12*, 99
pre-formal reading 88–89
print referencing 31, *75*
processing, stages of 79–82; and the use of symbols 83–84

"Queen's Jubilee, The" (story) 38

reading 4–5, 7–8; and changes faced by special schools 11–13; current thinking 10–11; and the curriculum framework 14–18; and the engagement model 13–14; importance of 9–10; inclusive view of 21–24; reading framework 24–29, *24*, 70; science of 54–56, *55*; stages of processing 79–82, *80*; *see also* difficulty learning to read; inclusive reading curriculum; literacy; reading, development of; reading, teaching of

reading, development of 53–54, 56–57, *56*, *87*; foundation skills 58–63; and learners with complex needs 57–58; and the Reading Rope 57–58; and the science of reading 54–56

reading, teaching of 65–66; and auditory discrimination 70; and the importance of sound 69–70; and orthographic mapping 74–76; and phonics 67, 72–74, 76; and phonological awareness 67–69; and a rich literacy environment 70–72; where to begin 66–67

reading policy 88–89

Reading Rope 57–58, *57*, *92*

reading spines 40–41

reference books 42

regular structured literacy opportunities 25, 94

relationships 28

repetition 106; repetitive texts 41

research 16

rhyming 69–70

rhythm 62

rich literacy environment *see* environments, literacy-rich

schools: reading spines for 40–41; *see also* special schools

science of reading 54–56, *55*

semi-formal curriculum pathway 99–100

sensory stories 35–39, 42, 59–60, *96*, 103–104

shared understanding 88–89

Sheffield, Nick 14, 15

sight words 72; sight word learning 94–96

social media opportunities 41

sound: discrimination 62; importance of 69–70

special schools 90, 95, 96–97; and accessible literacy-rich environments 32–35, 39–40, 42–45, 50, 51; curriculum pathways at 13; and difficulty learning to read 83–84; and high expectations 22, 23–24, 26, 28; and phonics 66, 70–71, 74–75; and planning 99–100, 102; and prioritising reading 3, 15–16, 17; and reading development 53–54, 63; reading policy 88–89

stories 105; community of story sharers 34; Jonathan 22–24, *22*; making your own books 34–39, *36*; sensory 35–39; sharing stories 33–34, 94; story boards 42; story books 41; story massage 42; story mats 42

structured literacy opportunities 25

structured synthetic phonics programme (SSP) 100–101

support, strategies to: and four stages of processing 79–82; and the use of symbols 83–84

symbols 83–84

teaching 65–66; and auditory discrimination 70; foundations of literacy 12; and the importance of sound 69–70; and orthographic mapping 74–76; and phonics 67, 72–74, 76, 98, 100–101; and phonological awareness 67–69; and a rich literacy environment 70–72; where to begin 66–67

technology *see* assistive technology

text: core texts 96–98; creating collections 41–42; creating and sharing across the school 49; engaging and accessible 39–40; high-quality 40–41

understanding: of how reading develops 24–25, 103; shared 88–89

visual pathways 39, 73, *73*

Wells, Pete 103–104

whole word: phonics vs. 72–74, *73*; whole-word learning 73

wordless/picture books 41

word recognition 25, 92–93

working memory 62–63, 81–82

For Product Safety Concerns and Information please contact our EU representative GPSR@taylorandfrancis.com
Taylor & Francis Verlag GmbH, Kaufingerstraße 24, 80331 München, Germany

www.ingramcontent.com/pod-product-compliance
Lightning Source LLC
Chambersburg PA
CBHW082004220426
43668CB00015B/2204